Essential Landscaping

IDEAS & PROJECTS

Essential Landscaping

This Old House® Books

EDITORIAL DIRECTOR Paul Spring

Development Team

EDITOR Mark Feirer
ART DIRECTOR Sue Ng
HORTICULTURAL CONSULTANT Lynn Ocone
PHOTO EDITOR Susan Sung Danelian
COPY EDITOR Steven H. Saltzman
PRODUCTION COORDINATOR Robert Hardin

Special thanks to: Joseph Greco, Anthony Wendling, Joseph Milidantri

PRESIDENT Rob Gursha
VICE PRESIDENT, BRANDED BUSINESSES David Arfine
EXECUTIVE DIRECTOR, MARKETING SERVICES Carol Pittard
DIRECTOR, RETAIL & SPECIAL SALES Tom Mifsud
DIRECTOR OF FINANCE Tricia Griffin
MARKETING DIRECTOR Kenneth Maehlum
PREPRESS MANAGER Emily Rabin
ASSOCIATE PRODUCT MANAGER Sara Stumpf
ASSISTANT PRODUCT MANAGER Linda Frisbie

Special thanks to: Suzanne DeBenedetto, Robert Dente, Gina Di Meglio, Ann-Michelle Gallero, Peter Harper, Natalie McCrea, Jessica McGrath, Jonathan Polsky, Mary Jane Rigoroso, Steven Sandonato, Bozena Szwagulinski, Niki Whelan

Published by

This Old House Ventures, Inc.
1185 Avenue of the Americas
New York, NY 10036

First Edition
ISBN: 1-931933-18-9
Library of Congress Catalogue Number: 2002102253

We welcome your comments and suggestions about *This Old House* books. Please write to us at:
This Old House Books
Attention: Book Editors
P.O. Box 11016
Des Moines, IA 50336-1016

If you would like to order any of the *This Old House* books, please call us at 1-800-327-6388.

First Edition, ISBN 1-931933-18-9

Contents

Yard D

esign Basics

NEW WAYS TO LOOK AT YOUR LANDSCAPE

FACED WITH A BEWILDERING VARIETY OF PLANTS AND OUT-door materials, it's no surprise that newcomers to landscape design soon discover that the hardest part comes right up front: planning the project. In fact, there's a nearly inpenetrable thicket of questions to hack through even if the whole thing is in the hands of an experienced land-scape designer. To make sense of it all, get a grip on the basics and don't get bogged down in minutiae. The following pages won't turn you into a design expert, but they'll get you start-ed and, we hope, inspire you to think about all the possibilities ahead.

Design Concepts For Great Yards

Keep an eye on the big picture and mimimize your maintenance chores

A WELL-LANDSCAPED PROPERTY ISN'T JUST ABOUT planting—it's every bit as much about planning. That's not just deciding where to dig holes for Saturday's hurried harvest of potted nursery plants. Instead, step back and consider your house as well as the land it sits on. By considering changes to both as part of your overall plan, you'll be more likely to end up with a scheme that captures your imagination.

If architecture often inspires landscaping, what better place to look for inspiration at the front of the house. A portico, for example, is to a house what manners were to Emily Post: thoughtfulness incarnate, a permanent umbrella ready to shelter guests as you greet them at the front door. At its most basic, a portico is simply a roof supported by columns. Add a bench and railings, and it becomes a waystation where you can sit down to pull off your boots before heading indoors, or an oasis from which you can regard the neighborhood at day's end. When architect James Widder first saw his client's 1908 Craftsman-style, stucco-faced house (photo, right), it was fronted by a dark porch with little curb appeal. His solution: Replace it with a new, more neighborly porch, featuring a central gable supported by redwood columns and concrete-block piers faced with brick.

A backyard is another location where architecture and landscape often collaborate. Hilary and Steve Chasin weren't looking for the usual real estate selling points when they were house hunting. "Basicallly," says Hilary, "we wanted a screened porch with a house attached." The house they finally fell in love with didn't have one, so they added it (bottom photo, facing page). The design mirrors porportions of an existing kitchen bump-out on the other end of the house. Fully screened walls bring the landscape closer. "When you're in there," says Hilary, "the grass is right next to you, and the flowers are within smelling distance."

PLANT DESIGN BASICS

Some yards seem almost as if they grew without human intervention. But landscape architects John Geiger and Dawn Handler point out that, just like a formal garden, a casual, naturalistic landscape must be based on clear-cut principles.

Eaves that echo the roof pitch of the main house help this portico addition blend in. New landscaping completes the scene.

KAREN MELVIN

SAXON HOLT

The visually-light wooden gates of this entry garden allow a glimpse of the scenery beyond.

JOHN BLAIS

This screened porch anchors a newly landscaped yard and patio. Its slate roof matches that of the house, helping the new addition to blend in.

"Trees come first in a landscape plan," says Geiger. "You can use them to develop a woodland walkway, a meditation space, a formal garden, a children's area, all on one site." For added interest, combine lower growing shrubs, perennials, and ground covers with trees. Shorter plants usually go nearer to roads and open spaces, and in front of taller varieties.

Plant density also matters. "Open plants work best in the foreground, with the denser plants such as upright junipers, providing the backdrop," Handler says. In fact, says Geiger, insufficient planting is a common mistake. "Instead of planting one or two of something, it's usually better to put in five or six of the same species, so that one plant group gently flows into another." This massing also yields a practical advantage: Dense foliage can minimize weed growth and the need for repeated mulching.

Many gardens look fabulous in spring, then drab for the next 10 months, so Geiger and Handler choose plants to create a year-round sequence of color. Daffodils and witch hazel will bloom in early spring, followed by azaleas, rhododendrons, and dogwoods in May and June. In late June through August, hydrangeas, spireas, butterfly bushes, and shrub roses will flower; then in the fall, sweet gum, burning bush, and Korean Stewartia trees will provide crimson foliage. Even in winter, says Handler, the red gnome Siberian dogwood will look fabulous against the snow.

But having a breathtaking yard doesn't mean you always have to be out of breath from maintaining it. You can enjoy lush, green grass with less effort. And it's even possible to have colorful flowers, trees, and shrubs without spending much of your life watering, weeding and pruning. The key is working smarter, not harder. The following labor-saving tactics target the three yard areas you spend the most time on: lawn, flower beds, and permanent plants.

LOSE SOME LAWN

Big lawns are dear to the heart of American homeowners, but lawn is an extremely labor-intensive landscape. You can reduce yard maintenance by removing a portion of the lawn and replacing it with functional, low-maintenance surfaces, such as wood decking, a brick patio, or gravel paths. Or you can put in a range of permanent landscape plants that will slice hours off your weekly maintenance routine.

Be smart about the lawn you have left. Design

In this small garden, brick paving eliminates the need for a lawn that would be awkward to care for.

SAXON HOLT

it so you can mow without stopping and backing up constantly. Connect lawn areas instead of planting in patches, and avoid sharp curves and corners—they're harder to mow than straight or gently curving lines. Don't set paving stones in grass, either, or you'll struggle to keep them clear. And avoid cross- and uphill mowing by not planting grass on slopes. Instead, plant no-mow ground covers, such as cotoneaster or juniper, on sloped areas. Consider the following as well:

• Size grass paths conveniently. With a standard 21-inch mower you can easily mow a path 36 to 40 inches wide in two passes without leaving a narrow unmowed strip.

• Put mailboxes, boulders, lampposts, and other impediments in a planting bed where they're out of the way.

• If you remove low-hanging tree branches, you won't have to duck as you mow under them.

• Install concrete or brick mowing strips at the edge of the lawn, level with the soil. Mower wheels ride on top of the strip so blades cut edge and grass in one pass.

• Reduce raking and fertilizing by using a mulching mower to hide clippings in the grass. Don't worry—clippings don't cause thatch. And because they feed the lawn as they decompose, clippings reduce the amount of supplemental fertilizer the lawn needs by 20 to 30 percent.

FINESSE THE FLOWERS

Annuals and perennials produce more color per square foot than other plants. But they also require more work. Annuals need yearly planting and removal, while perennials require occasional dividing and replanting. Both demand periodic fertilizing, watering, and weeding. Planting for impact and not quantity will maximize color while leaving you the time to enjoy it. Some of the liveliest gardens contain just one clump of well-placed flowers. Plants concentrated in a small bed require less maintenance than an equal number scattered about. Also:

• Plant flowers for maximum impact. High-visibility spots include the front entranceway, walkway borders and the edges of a deck.

• Highlight flowers by planting them in a raised bed or against a backdrop of green foliage.

• Use fewer varieties. A mass planting of one variety, such as annual impatiens or perennial coreopsis, can be just as appealing as a mixture of plants, and it's much easier to maintain.

• Avoid tall-growing plants that need to be staked, such as delphiniums and hollyhocks.

• Choose varieties that don't require pruning or deadheading. Traditional multiflora and grandi-

flora types of petunias, for example, stretch out by midsummer and bear few flowers unless pruned back. In contrast, some petunias, such as the trailing types and the compact Fantasy strain, bloom continuously without pruning.

• Make your flower beds narrow enough for easy reach. A bed that's wider than 2½ feet can be difficult to work from only one side.

• Install edging strips of metal, plastic, wood, or brick between beds and lawn. Edging keeps lawn grasses from invading flower beds and prevents soil from washing out over the lawn.

• Spread mulch over the soil surface between plants. Because mulch slows water evaporation from the soil by 30 to 70 percent, you won't have to irrigate as frequently. Mulch also discourages weeds.

OPEN UP TO THE YARD

What good is a great yard, though, if you can't get at it? That's what Molly and Leon Banowetz discovered. As owners of a graphic design firm in Dallas, they tolerate long hours, demanding clients, and high-pressure deadlines. So when the workday is done, they seek refuge in their house.

But a short time after they bought it, some less-than-perfect features came to light. For one thing, two bulky central air-conditioning units sat outside the kitchen window, interfering with the view and filling the backyard with noise. To get from

ABOVE: **Adding French doors means cutting a hole in the house. Structural and waterproofing details are critical.**
RIGHT: **Unlike a patio door, French doors make the entire opening accessible, maximizing access to the deck.**

MICHAEL MANUEL (2)

the kitchen to the small back deck at the opposite end of the house, the couple had to go through the dining room, living room, and sunroom. And the dining room was dominated by a picture window with a beautiful view of the pool, but offered no way to get there. Worst of all, the kitchen storm door opened onto a narrow, concrete back stoop. Every time they carried in an armload of groceries or took trays of of food out to the pool, they were fumbling with the screen door.

Leon quickly conceived a solution: Build a new deck and replace the kitchen and dining room windows with French doors. "I really wanted to open up the back of this house and also make it more functional," he says.

After moving the air-conditioning compressors to the side of the house, the Banowetzes turned to a local contractor for the door installation. His crew took out the old windows and cut the wall down to where the deck would be. The doors themselves were hung in a day.

"This was a great investment," Leon said when workers completed the project. "It has totally changed the way we live. We eat outside more, and on weekends, if it's nice, we leave the doors open all day. Now the first thing visitors want to do is walk right into the backyard."

AND DO YOUR HOMEWORK

A terrific, low-maintenance landscape plan won't be worth much if you can't build it. As you develop ideas, particularly if they involve large, expensive features such as ponds, patios, or walls, make sure you own what you think you do. Municipalities usually require a survey before changes are made to a house's footprint and before hardscaping plans are implemented. This ensures that minimum zoning setbacks are met and the locations of lot lines are known. You may also need a permit for decks, ponds, or other features.

After checking whether your town requires such reconnaissance, you may have to hire a surveyor to collect deeds, plats (drawings from previous surveys), and zoning information from local government offices. He'll also map out the site. Once he's sure of the property lines, he stakes the boundaries and files a copy of the survey survey with the county government office.

Don't assume you know where your lot begins and ends. In Westchester County, New York, a woman took her real estate agent's word that her neighbors' fence defined the boundary between the two houses. Shortly after, she hired a tree service to cut down five mature spruce trees on her side to get more sunlight in her dining room.

FRAN BRENNAN

ABOVE: A low wall capped by smooth stone is a seating magnet for guests.
LEFT: The textural contrast between this small, rectangular pond and the nearby bluestone patio adds interest to a private garden.

Unfortunately, the actual property line extended 15 feet beyond her neighbors' fence, and the trees belonged to them. To avoid legal action, the now chastened homeowner paid for the installation of a dozen 12-foot-tall Norway spruces—at a cost of $6,000.

Along with knowing your lot boundaries, find out if any easements affect the area you wish to improve. An easement grants someone besides the property owner the right to use or pass over a specified part of the land for a particular purpose. Many residential utility easements run along property lines or encroach on lots. They allow utility companies to install and maintain cables, pipes, and poles.

Most utility easements exist in perpetuity, while other easements may have a limited life. Either way, home buyers should find out about easements on a property before they unknowingly build on, block access to, or improperly use land on which an easement exists. Even landscaping an easement area is risky, says real estate lawyer James V. Magee: "I know of cases where tree houses and fences had to be pulled down during utility repairs, gardens were destroyed, and pools moved. All at the owners' expense."

SAXON HOLT

View From The Curb

An attractive front yard improves the look of your home and makes visitors feel welcome

EVEN A GREAT FRONT YARD WON'T CHANGE YOUR LIFE, but it can lift your spirits each time you come home. Simple things, like a pleasant walk to the front door and a bit of relief from street traffic, can make a big difference in how you think about your home.

Most homeowners don't start with an ideal yard. Far from it. Some inherit a virtually blank slate, while others get an outdated yard with a standard-issue narrow walkway, a touch of shrubbery, and maybe a stingy concrete slab at the door. But reworking the front of a house can be intimidating—after all, everyone who passes by will have a chance to judge your efforts. So think of eliminating a dreary entrance as an opportunity not only to improve the look of a house but also to complement the neighborhood. Here are several success stories.

LUSH, LOW-WATER-USE LANDSCAPE

Starting from scratch, a couple in Austin, Texas, created a flourishing landscape (photo, right), that earned them a "Best New Xeriscape Award" for low water use from the city.

The couple wanted a Xeriscape garden but with plenty of color and a profusion of greenery, not a desert look. And they wanted more time to travel, so low-maintenance plantings were a priority. The chief challenge was soil hard as concrete, a local phenomena known as caliche. Intense summer heat and deer were other problems they had to contend with.

First, the couple developed an overall plan, which called for professional help designing and installing the mortared limestone paths and sprinkler system. They decided to leave existing boulders in place as features of the new landscape. The couple then turned to improving the soil, mixing truckloads of compost and other organic amendments into it. They mounded the improved soil in raised planting beds to provide extra depth for plant roots. As continuing maintenance, they spread shredded bark mulch 3 inches deep over the soil surface, which helps the soil remain cool and retain moisture.

Wise plant choices are central to the success of any garden. Jan, then a beginning gardener, learned about drought-resistant plants from a local garden club. And she experimented. "I didn't have an exact planting plan. Instead, I planted on an ad-hoc basis," she says. Among her many successes are shrubby

A practical design for low water use and minimal maintenance combines a small buffalo grass lawn with beds of drought-tolerant perennials and ornamental grasses.

KAREN BUSSOLINI

TIM THOELECKE

perennials, including lantana, autumn sage (*Salvia greggii*), and Mexican bush sage (*Salvia leucantha*). They provide rich color, and the deer that regularly browse their yard leave these alone.

The decision to limit the amount of turf and plant native, drought-resistant buffalo grass also saves water and reduces maintenance. This easy-care approach ensures that time spent in the yard is as pleasurable as possible.

THE POSSIBLE DREAM
With help from a landscape designer, a couple in Park Ridge, Illinois, were able to gain some privacy and space for parking by replacing their do-nothing front lawn.

"Originally, the house stood out like a big gray shoe box," recalls Barbara. The couple wanted it to blend in with the surroundings. They also needed parking space because the house had no driveway, which forced guests to park on the busy street. Some buffering from the street and low maintenance were other top priorities. "We like to spend time outdoors, but we're not gardeners," Barbara adds.

A new U-shaped driveway provides needed off-street parking. The planting beds in front of the drive add privacy to the front entry.

Landscape designer Tim Thoelecke, of Garden Concepts in Glenview, Illinois, put every inch of the 23-foot-deep site to work. He eliminated the front lawn and concrete walk and replaced them with an 11-foot-wide U-shaped driveway. "Now, people can park off the street, and don't have to back out into heavy traffic," Thoelecke says. The interlocking concrete pavers provide an easy-care surface compared with the lawn they replaced.

Thoelecke replaced the original foundation plantings—a single row of clipped shrubs pressed against the house—with deep planting beds for a generous look more in scale with the house.

New plantings are simple but hardworking. Amelanchier shrubs, shown above in spring flower, look good all year. Blossoms are followed in early summer by purplish berries; colorful fall foliage drops to reveal a striking silhouette in winter. The amelanchiers combine with lower-growing evergreens, ornamental grasses, and flowering bulbs to soften the transition from the house to the ground.

A planting bed next to the sidewalk includes a bench and creates a sense of enclosure. In summer, ornamental grasses planted behind the bench grow tall enough to screen it from the street. "I frequently sit out on the bench or the front stoop simply to enjoy the yard," says Barbara.

SMALL SPACE, BIG GARDEN

Homeowner Tom Mannion proved you don't need a big yard to make a big difference. He transformed his 30×100-foot front yard in Arlington, Virginia, into a gardener's dream. Granted, he had an advantage—Mannion is a professional landscape designer—but the solution he devised is far from esoteric.

"The yard felt like it belonged to the street, not the house," says Mannion. That's what happens when the lawn bleeds into the street and neighboring yards, he explains. The primary goals of the redesign were to reclaim the yard and make it welcoming to visitors. "I wanted a little privacy and a fun place to garden," Mannion says.

As the first task, the narrow stone path was torn up and replaced with a 6-foot-wide walkway that gently curves away toward the driveway. "I believe in wide walks," says Mannion. "They are more welcoming, and people can walk side by side instead of single file."

The new paving is exposed aggregate concrete with a pea-gravel finish. Both the walk and stoop are edged with the same type of stone used on the house. "It's important to pick up something from the house and repeat it in the landscape," says Mannion. This unifies the house and garden.

Just as Mannion advises his clients, he shaped the lawn first and then formed the surrounding planting beds. "Don't simply plant in the lawn," he says, "or it loses its shape and becomes nothing more than strips of connecting greenery."

A small garden bed featuring azaleas, spring-blooming doublefile viburnums, and winter-blooming hellebores separates the lawn and the street. The plants screen the yard while offering anyone walking past a view to enjoy.

Mannion planted a number of colorful annual flowers and bulbs at the doorway to greet visitors as they arrive. "Replanting this limited area in spring and fall is a seasonal gardening chore that I enjoy, but I kept it small," Mannion explains. "An area that's too large would be too much work." ■

A blooming crabapple was left in place, but a planting area was added around it. Spring bulbs at the front door are replaced after they flower by summer annuals.

ROGER FOLEY

Growth Spurts

How to make a major landscape job manageable by staging the work over a period of several years

OR MONIQUE AND CHRIS ALLEN—LANDSCAPE DESIGNER and horticulturist, respectively—a barren yard is a field of possibilities: They imagine vibrant islands of color and meandering pathways that help nestle a house into its setting and offer intriguing views in every season. It's no surprise that when the Allens went house hunting in Franklin, Massachusetts, back in 1997, it was the 2½-acre property—not the Cape Cod it surrounded—that attracted their attention. As their real estate agent sorted through a giant key ring and walked toward the front door, they didn't

At first, the house sat on the land "like a peanut." Bringing in top-soil gave the yard contours, making the diminutive Cape Cod look larger, and provided rich earth for new plantings.

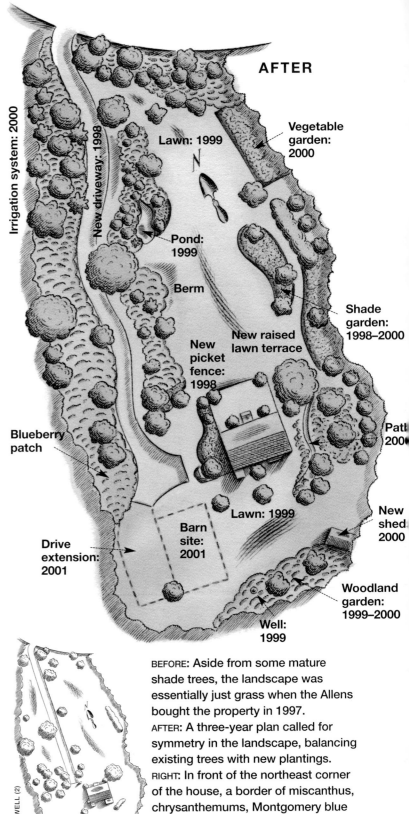

AFTER

Irrigation system: 2000

New driveway: 1998

Lawn: 1999

Vegetable garden: 2000

Pond: 1999

Berm

Shade garden: 1998–2000

New raised lawn terrace

New picket fence: 1998

Blueberry patch

Path 200

Drive extension: 2001

Barn site: 2001

Lawn: 1999

New shed 2000

Well: 1999

Woodland garden: 1999–2000

BEFORE

ANTHONY SIDWELL (2)

BEFORE: Aside from some mature shade trees, the landscape was essentially just grass when the Allens bought the property in 1997.

AFTER: A three-year plan called for symmetry in the landscape, balancing existing trees with new plantings.

RIGHT: In front of the northeast corner of the house, a border of miscanthus, chrysanthemums, Montgomery blue spruce, and a snowbell creates visual appeal with staggered heights, differing textures, and a variety of color.

BELOW: To create a focal point at the back of the land, Chris planted a multistemmed river birch, part of a woodland garden to be finished the next year.

ABOVE: Creating the shade garden was a three-stage process. In the first, Chris prepped the soil and relocated two dogwoods from beside the driveway.
BELOW: The next summer, the Allens added shrubs and trees.

follow her. Instead, they began exploring the land. "It had such great potential," says Monique. "We were like kids in a candy store." By the time the couple looked inside the 1980 house, their minds were all but made up. "Short of finding the place condemned, we were going to buy it," she admits.

Before the Allens even moved in, they began devising a master plan for the property. They would transform the uninteresting field into an inviting dreamworld, complete with a fishpond, lots of perennial gardens, and a new driveway. An overhaul of such magnitude was well beyond their immediate means, so they broke the job into three phases, with the intention of biting off manageable chunks over a three-year period. Staging a landscape project in multiple phases is something Monique frequently does for her clients, and she heartily recommends it even when the budget can handle doing everything in a single season. "The genius of a multistage plan is that over time, you have the leisure to change, enrich, and broaden your ideas," says Monique, who counts *This Old House*'s Norm Abram, Steve Thomas, and Richard Trethewey as regular customers. She likens the experience to moving into a house. "It takes time to get accustomed to the place," she says. "Once you've lived there for a while and you're familiar with its strengths and shortcomings, you may decide to turn a window into French doors, move a stairway, or make other

and establishes a timetable for each, says Monique. Like a typical single-phase project, the job should proceed from large site work (earthmoving, a new driveway, relocating existing trees) to the creation of focal points (ponds, gardens, walls) and finally to planting (perennial beds, spring bulbs, hedgerows). And while the entire scheme is carried out over a number of years, each distinct job should be completed in the same season it starts. Determining the scope of individual phases is a matter of budget; the Allens broke their project into three essentially equal chunks.

YEAR 1: EARTH SHAPING AND DRAINAGE

Monique calls the work that she did the first summer "structural," an apt metaphor for topographic changes. "We had 300 feet of road frontage, with the house sitting on the land like a peanut," she says (photo, page 20). "We wanted to make the building seem bigger by defining a smaller space around it." So the Allens raised the grade over a 24-by-36-foot area in front of the house (two times the footprint of the building is the proper proportion, she says) and enclosed it with a picket fence to create a distinct front yard.

Next they turned to the 30-foot-long driveway. "It was straight as a runway, right down the middle of the property, and chopped the landscape into two pieces," she says. They removed it and created a graceful, curving gravel track along the side of the property. Then they partially screened it from the house by creating sloping mounds, called berms, along its edge and in other key spots throughout the landscape. This required a bulldozer and 300 cubic yards of topsoil, and the work proceeded from the back of the property to the front— "a good idea so that you don't paint yourself into a corner and have to drive machinery over your work," Monique says. In other words, resist the urge to start in the front yard. The berms gave the land a variety of heights and forms, offering more features to catch the eye and more intimate spaces where people can interact with nature.

Although the Allens' landscape didn't have drainage problems, berms can also help alleviate such issues because water flows down and away from elevated areas. Always improve drainage as part of the first stage. "Most plants don't like soggy soil," says Monique, "and dealing with the problem later would mean tearing up landscaping you've already installed." If grading isn't sufficient, drywells might be in order. And any work that will disrupt other parts of the yard because of heavy equipment should be conducted in the first stage,

changes so the space suits you. It's the same learning process with the yard."

Still, as all projects should, this one started with a vision for what the landscape could become—albeit a flexible one. "You need to dream before you start moving earth around," says Monique. "Dreams are cheap. Moving earth is expensive." To begin developing a plan, she advises her clients to tear appealing pictures out of home and garden magazines. "Pin them up on a bulletin board and create a visual buffet of ideas," she says. Then see what recurs—those features will be the ones you want. "I had a client who did this, and every photo she pinned up included cobblestones. She hadn't even thought about cobblestones before." Allen also recommends looking at other properties for ideas. Then, preferably with the help of a professional, these fantasies can be turned into a strategy that breaks the work into individual stages

Finally, the Allens filled in spots between the trees and shrubs with low-light plants and created a gravel path (this view is toward the back of the property).

says Monique. That includes removing dead trees and planting large shade trees (considered anything larger than 30 feet).

YEAR 2: FOCAL POINTS

The following year, Monique and Chris created the focal points of their landscape, including a pond, clusters of ornamental trees (typically under 30 feet tall), a blueberry patch, and a vegetable garden. "Over time we found that when we walked the land, we'd go back to the same places again and again." They located the "vignettes" in these especially appealing spots.

They also found a way to bring to life the least-used part of the property—the wooded east side of the house. "Every landscape has at least one of these underutilized spots," says Monique, "and following a multistage plan gives you the chance to find it." The Allens turned their forgotten shady spot into a garden of low-light plantings. They had transplanted a few ornamental trees into the location in phase one, but in phase two, they transformed the space completely. "We felt that would entice us to journey there." They filled the space with Japanese forest grass, dogwoods, rhododendrons, and mountain laurel—low-light grasses and shrubs that won't have to be pruned in this naturalistic setting. In phase three they planted the floor of the garden with lusciously textured groundcovers and bold perennials and laid a meandering path. "People think that in order to have a colorful garden, you need a sunny location," she says, "but shade gardens can offer incredibly vibrant hues and lush textures."

For the pond, the Allens excavated an 11- by 22-foot hole under the protective shade of a large existing pear tree that can be seen from the front windows. After laying a rubber liner into the depression, they surrounded the top edge with half-buried stones to make it look like it was a natural feature of the landscape. A 3- by 6-foot "header" pond at the top of a berm feeds a waterfall into the larger pond. "The meditative aspects of a pond are phenomenal. Water gives a sense of peace to a landscape. And a pond is a little ecosystem all to itself." They stocked it with goldfish and flowering plants, but the frogs came on their own. Other focal points Monique advises homeowners to install in stage two include structures such as gazebos, arbors, pergolas, latticework, statuary, and large bolders.

YEAR 3: FINALLY, THE PLANTS

It was their third year in the house when the two gardeners finally let themselves order vast quantities of ornamental trees and shrubs, perennials, and groundcovers. By creating interesting combi-

nations of plantings in a variety of colors, shapes, and sizes, the Allens screened the driveway and neighboring house and brought the landscape to life. "When we graded the land in the first year, we moved some of the existing trees to spots along and behind the berms," Monique says. "Now we filled in spaces between them with new plantings. We used to be able to see the street and neighbor's property; now we don't see any property but our own from the house."

The Allens chose plants that would provide interesting views in every season. For winter they planted 'Heritage' river birches with beautiful, peeling pinkish-tan bark, paperbark maples, twisty Japanese maples, winterberries, and many ornamental grasses with seedhead plumes. They put in

TOP LEFT: **Lawn provides an open space in the landscape and contrasts with adjacent landscape plants.**
BOTTOM LEFT: **A rock border hides the pond liner; the fiberglass basin was connected to the main one by a waterfall and a pump. When planted with lush, colorful plants, the pond became a favorite hangout for Monique and husband Chris, above.**

dogwoods for spring flowers and fall berries, summer-blooming azaleas and itea for summer interest, along with stewartias, a sourwood tree, and a franklinia that flowers in the fall. They also added weeping birch and cherry, plus two hemlocks, plantings that would "provide movement and grace all year," says Monique.

No sooner had the couple completed their three-year landscaping project than they began making new and ambitious plans. With obvious excitement in her voice, Monique described a retaining wall along the edge of the front yard and a new barn. Year 4 will surely bring yet another stage of this project, and the landscape will keep evolving. "A gardener is never done gardening," she says.

Eliminating A Lawn

You'll discover a wealth of opportunities if you cut your maintenance instead of the grass

A BURGEONING NUMBER OF HOMEOWNERS ACROSS THE country are reducing—or even eradicating—their lawns in favor of landscaping schemes that require less time and trouble to maintain. "It's happening as people realize that they don't want to spend their weekends mowing a lawn," notes master gardener Janet Marinelli, author of *Stalking the Wild Amaranth: Gardening in the Age of Extinction* and director of publishing at the Brooklyn Botanic Garden. Also fueling the trend, adds Marinelli, are water restrictions being imposed in dry regions and increasing interest in using native plants to create habitats that attract birds, butterflies, and other wildlife.

The turf lawn has been part of the American landscape since colonial days, when the wealthy transplanted the idea from England. But since the grasses tend to be nonnative species, maintaining them generally requires lots of water and at least some chemical intervention: herbicides, fertilizers, and pesticides. Of course, natural lawn-care tactics (composting clippings, aerating the soil, and weeding by hand) and learning to live without putting-green perfection can go a long way toward reducing chemical dependency. But lawns still gobble up hours.

Enter alternative approaches that are becoming more and more mainstream. "There are lots of attractive landscaping solutions for the front yard that can give homeowners more satisfaction and pleasure than traditional turf," says Marinelli.

For painter Jean Gordon, a field of flowers offers artistic inspiration as well as everyday beauty. Her meadowlike flower garden took root as lawn care became more frustrating. At first, a bluestone walk with border beds bisected the green turf and, says Gordon, "each spring I made the border beds a bit bigger so there was less grass to tend." The last straw came when her lawn was infested with destructive chinch bugs. Rather than replace the sickly sod, she dug it all out with a hand fork. "Everything is helter-skelter—a mix of annuals and perennials of varying height, color, and foliage," she notes. She packs in as many plants as the space can hold, and estimates that the small plot is brimming with 40 different types of flowers, all chosen with one criterion: "I plant what I love to paint."

The idea behind another lawn-gone garden is the opposite of a sun-loving showcase for flowers. Washington, D.C., landscape architect Wolfgang Oehme, famous for his naturalistic work,

A mix of drought tolerant groundcovers and perennials is a practical alternative to lawn.

SAXON HOLT

MICHAEL MᴄCASKEY

saw the inherent possibilities of his client's shady suburban site where turf couldn't thrive. He suggested supplanting the lawn in front of her house with an asymmetrical layering of plant material that would simulate a natural woodland: low ground covers like lily turf, hostas, barrenwort, and Lenten rose mingling with midsize Chinese dogwood, clumping bamboo, and holly—all

Turf may not be an option in desert regions, but a variety of native plants can make a beautiful front yard.

designed to blend with the lofty sweetgum, magnolia, and other trees on the site. "It's an elegant space where varied shades and textures of green foliage are punctuated with flowers here and there." Oehme's vision treats the yard as a private room, shielding the house from the street and providing changing views year-round from his client's dining room window.

Hardscape strategies incorporating patios and benches offer another approach to the unlawn. When the owners of an English Country–style house outside Minneapolis first approached landscape designer Carter Clapsadle, they asked him to take their humdrum 20-by-40-foot front yard with its overgrown evergreens and cold concrete walk and "just make it beautiful." Their children now grown, the owners wanted to transform their home into an oasis with outdoor space for entertaining. Taking his inspiration from the home's thick cedar-shake roof, sage-green shutters, and grayish-pink stucco, he envisioned a charming stone cottage in the lush British countryside—but without a blade of grass in sight.

LEFT: Roger Cook uses a sod cutter set to a depth of 1½ to 2 inches to remove a lawn. Then he uses a garden edger (BELOW LEFT) to slice it into manageable 6-foot sections before rolling them up. Healthy turf removed from a lawn can be transplanted elsewhere.

KINDRA CLINEFF (3)

MICHAEL MacCASKEY

Staggered pavers and drought-tolerant plantings replaced lawn and a strip of concrete.

With unkempt junipers and yews and a gangly maple staggered in front of the house, plus a sterile walkway leading from the driveway along the facade, the scruffy—and inconvenient— approach to the front door presented an off-putting obstacle course, says Clapsadle. "You had to maneuver around these big shrubs, so everyone, including the mailman, used the side or back entrances," he recalls. Plus, the home faced a spectacular pond view that was blocked by a hedge of towering arborvitae.

Clapsadle's plan called for getting rid of the concrete path and creating a 550-square-foot bluestone terrace extending 25 feet out from the house. Flower beds create a soft border around its hard, zigzag edge, and terraced steps lead up to the entryway. Careful pruning of the arborvitae cleared a "window view" from house to pond, and a 10-by-12-foot, 9-foot-high pergola furnished with an outdoor table and benches creates a living room overlooking the pond. The owners sit there in the morning and sip their coffee, and have friends over for cocktails in the evening. "Not only does the house look like it could be in the Cotswolds," says Clapsadle, "but everyone, even the mailman, uses the front entrance. And my clients finally have their outdoor oasis." ◼

Planting for Privacy

Turn your yard into a secluded haven without giving your neighbors the cold shoulder

TOTAL PRIVACY—IT'S EASY TO ACHIEVE, AS LONG AS YOU don't mind an 8-foot-high stone wall surrounding your property. If that sounds a little too much like a fortress, there are less drastic options to choose from, ranging from vine-covered fencing to informal and even fragrant hedges. When providing privacy is the primary goal of a landscape plan, try to create a buffer that's beautiful as well as neighborly. To get it, you can use plants or fencing, or best of all, a combination of the two.

PRIVACY FENCING

A fence goes up fast, providing instant privacy. And if you choose materials well and build it carefully, a fence is relatively easy to maintain and will last for decades. It will also do a good job of keeping strangers out and kids and pets in. Fencing is space efficient, too; a 6-foot-high fence takes up only 10 to 12 inches of ground space. Plus, with so many styles and materials to choose from, you can easily match your fence to your home and other landscape features.

But fencing comes with some disadvantages. Surrounding yourself with a solid fence creates a boxed-in feeling, particularly in a small yard. What's more, local zoning ordinances often limit the height and location of perimeter fences. And a fence constructed at the maximum allowable height might not be sufficient to screen views from the neighbors' second-story windows. Fencing costs add up quickly, even if you save 40 to 50 percent buying the materials and building the fence yourself.

Select the fence style carefully (see pages 118–121). A solid-board fence blocks the view completely but it cuts out light and breezes. Open fences, such as those with louvers and lattice panels, are friendlier and more comfortable, and will also make the yard feel larger. They combine beautifully with plants, serving double duty as privacy screen and vine support.

You might not need to surround your entire yard to gain privacy. Short sections of fence placed at strategic locations in the yard may be all that's needed to screen a sitting area, patio, or deck. This cuts the expense and effort of a full-length fence, and creates separate outdoor "rooms" that can result in a more livable yard overall. Keep interior fencing as low as possible,

A vine-shaded seating area offers an oasis of privacy. Plants soften the hard edges of the woodwork.

SAXON HOLT

however, or it will feel intrusive and cast too much shade on adjacent plants. (For more on fencing, see page 116).

TREES AND SHRUBS

There's no substitute for the natural beauty plants provide. They are usually less expensive than fences and are rarely limited by local codes. What's more, some trees and shrubs can do a better job of reducing dust and noise than a fence.

Alas, a living privacy screen isn't always a perfect solution, either. Trees and shrubs take time to mature, so they usually don't provide immediate privacy. And they require much more ground space than a fence. A narrow hedge requires a minimum of 3 feet, while some hedge plants spread horizontally a distance of 8 feet or more. And even low-maintenance plants require routine watering, weeding, and mulching.

Still, there are lots of ways to make trees and shrubs work to your advantage when you want to be alone. Hedges are what many people think of first. A hedge is a single line of plants, usually all the same variety. A formal hedge is clipped or sheared—often several times during a growing season—to maintain a particular size and shape. But with a lot less work you can have an informal hedge by choosing plants that will naturally stay the height and width you want without the demands of clipping.

Consider the following basics if a hedge figures into your plans. First, decide between deciduous and evergreen plants. Deciduous plants block views fully only in spring and summer while they're leafed out. A seasonal screen of this nature might be all that's required if you spend most of your time indoors in winter. Deciduous plants tend to grow faster than evergreens, which is an advantage when planting for privacy. And, as a general rule, you can space them farther apart, so fewer plants are required.

Evergreens, on the other hand, grow more densely and provide year-round privacy. They make the perfect backdrop for colorful flowers or a mixed shrub border.

When choosing plants for hedges, remember that an ideal privacy shrub has dense foliage from top to bottom. Also consider the ultimate height, spread and growth rate of the plants. Especially in places where ground space is limited, select varieties of trees and shrubs that naturally grow tall and narrow. The word *fastigiate* or *columnar* in the plant name indicates just such a growth form. For example, the fastigiate English oak grows 60 feet high but only 10 to 15 feet wide, compared

MICHAEL MacCASKEY

A weathered length of solid-board fence blocks neighbor's views and creates a cozy backdrop for seating. Leafy plants embrace both sides of the patio, increasing the intimacy of the space.

with the typical English oak that grows to 40 feet or more wide.

Planting for privacy doesn't have to mean growing a hedge. A casual grouping of different types of shrubs and trees can make an effective and often more interesting screen. For example, a handsome shrub trio that provides flowers and ornamental fruits includes beautybush, bayberry, and American highbush cranberry. If space allows, plant these shrubs in a zigzag pattern instead of in straight rows—the result will be a denser screen and a more interesting arrangement.

You can always fill in between slow-growing shrubs with large, temporary perennials and ornamental grasses.

Consider these additional ways to use shrubs and trees for privacy:

• Plant a row of waist-high shrubs, such as dwarf cranberry bush or dwarf Korean lilac, within a larger yard to enclose a swimming pool, patio, or deck.

• Alternate groups of plants with fence sections to create an open feeling and reduce the cost of fencing the yard.

• Plant a single tree that has horizontally spreading branches, such as mimosa, pagoda dogwood, or Chinese pistache, to block overhead views.

• Position a single tree or group of shrubs to break the line of sight in key locations. For example, use such a grouping to shield the front door from the street.

• Create a movable or temporary screen with shrubs or small trees planted in large containers. Container plants are especially useful on a deck or patio where there's no ground for gardening. Place containers on wheeled plant caddies for easy maneuvering and to protect decking from rot.

• Plant a row of tall, narrow shrubs or trees along an existing fence to add greater height to the privacy screen.

VINES

Vines provide a very effective living screen, yet they occupy very little ground space. Vines are especially useful when you need to divide a narrow space or create a barrier that won't get in the way of foot traffic.

Vines represent a good value for your money, too. A vigorous vine, such as golden hops or silver lace vine, costs about $20 in 1-gallon container, and each can cover 20 feet of fence in just a year or two. These and other fast-growing vines make a young landscape appear full and mature.

Vines turn even the most ordinary fence into a graceful backdrop of flowers and greenery. And when grown over an arbor, woody vines like wisteria and grape are an attractive way to block views from above into your yard, and at the same time they provide shade.

All vines need some sort of structure—a fence, trellis or arbor—on which to climb. Clinging vines, such

LEFT: Supported by an arbor, silky wisteria provides overhead privacy and shade. A simple color scheme of gray and white unites the fence, home, and vine.

as climbing hydrangea and Boston ivy, hold tight with suction cups or little rootlets, making these plants very difficult to remove from their supports. Clingers also have a deserved reputation for damaging the surface they rely upon for support, especially if it's made of wood. And, any dense vine grown directly on a fence interferes with paining and repairs.

Once established, vines can be aggressive, too. You'll need to keep your pruners sharp and use them freely. Select plants carefully and be sure any support is strong enough to bear the weight of the vine. It's no fun to watch a front porch trellis collapse under a big wisteria in its prime.

Just as with trees and shrubs, some vines are evergreen and others are deciduous. A deciduous vine planted over an arbor gives a bit of shade during the summer, but when leaves drop, you'll face good news and bad: Warming sunlight can penetrate but privacy will evaporate.

If you wish to break up the monotony of a standard 6-foot fence without completely smothering it, choose a vine that is both vigorous and easily controlled, such as *Clematis jackmanii*. This rapid grower reaches heights of 10 to 12 feet with a profusion of velvety purple summer flowers.

Clematis are among vines that climb by coiling their leafstalks around their support. They will scramble up a trellis or open-design fence with just a little prompting.

In contrast, a dense-growing vine, such as Boston ivy or silver lace vine, will smother a chain-link fence and create a complete visual barrier in the process. Remember, though, aggressive vines don't slow down with age, so they require plenty of space as well as serious pruning to keep them from getting out of control.

SIZING A SCREEN

It's hard to imagine just how high a fence or hedge will have to be in order to screen views into and out of the yard. Here's a simple method that will help you visualize the results. First, drive temporary stakes in the ground at the intended end points of the screen. The stakes should be as high as you expect the screen to be. Then string brightly colored plastic flagging tape (the thin, easy-to-work-with type available at hardware stores) across the top of the stakes. Now back away, walk around, and check out your screen prototype from various vantage points around the yard. Imagine how it will look—and work—in every season. Once you're satisfied, start planting. ■

An old-fashioned rose cloaking a sturdy arbor bursts into bloom in the spring.

SAXON HOLT

Entertaining Outdoors

With the right mix of materials and lighting, you can turn your backyard into an oasis of activity

With the advent of summer, everyone feels the urge to spend as much time outdoors as possible. Then, even workday evenings can feel like mini-vacations—especially when the outdoor space is furnished comfortably. Here are three very different approaches to providing the right mix of features for outdoor living.

AN ENTERTAINING COURTYARD

Stepping through the arched, mahogany-framed doors into Karen and Rob Cowan's stucco-faced courtyard (photos, this page), it's hard to imagine that none of this existed before. The Cowans had spent two years refurbishing the interior of their 1927 Mediterranean-style house in Los Angeles before undertaking the creation of an outdoor living area that would link the house to its setting. They found the space by removing a large, unappealing room—which turned out to be the original courtyard that a previous owner had enclosed.

Dismantling the old room was the first step in the reclamation. Workers tore out a wall of French doors as well as

RIGHT: An outdoor fireplace cancels the chill of cool nights. BELOW: Lighting extends outdoor living into the evening.

DAVID ALBANESE (2)

another wall that blocked off an outdoor staircase leading to the second floor. The only element remaining after the demolition was a well-positioned fireplace, which they stripped of its unsightly flagstone face. Ripping up the double-layer concrete foundation required a Bobcat with a hydraulic jack; the effort unearthed a star-shaped mark where a fountain once stood. The Cowans were interested in restoring a water element to the patio, but weren't sure they wanted to interrupt the open space. In the end, "Rob went to buy a small wall fountain and came back with this!" Karen says, pointing to a two-tiered stone fountain. It stands right on the spot where they found the old one's ghost.

Before installing the fountain, the Cowans positioned a 20-year-old, 25-foot jacaranda tree selected by their landscape architect, Steve Silva (no relation to *This Old House* contractor Tom), for its lacy canopy of purple flowers and tiny leaves, which casts dappled light onto the patio. Because of its size, the tree had to be hoisted into place by a crane. Next, Silva's crew dug trenches for the waterlines and drains that would service the fountain. Finally, Italian roof tiles, chosen for their patinated, terra-cotta tones, were laid down in a circle around the base of the fountain.

Lighting large outdoor spaces such as the Cowans' courtyard calls for more than candles and hurricane lamps. In fact, a terrace, patio, or deck should be lit with as much attention as an indoor room: that is, with ambient lighting; task lighting near work surfaces; mood lighting for atmosphere; and floods or spots for safety, which is especially important along paths and up steps leading to and from the outdoor area.

Lighting designers have a term for the overall plan of an outdoor space: lightscaping. The technique includes special effects such as up-lighting the foliage of a favorite tree; silhouetting, or spotlighting, an object such as a birdbath or sundial from behind and below; and cross-lighting, or dramatizing a specific object or planting by placing light fixtures in two or more places near it.

The American Lighting Association offers a few tips for initiating a lighting scheme. On a clear, moonlit night, walk around the area with a flashlight. Take note of where the moon shines brightest; these are the spots in which to place ambient lights to emulate moon glow. If dark areas occur near doors, they should be lit as a security measure. Beam your flashlight on spots you think you might want to dramatize; once you get a sense of how they'll look, highlight the areas with appropriate fixtures. As you make your plan, be con-

FRAN BRENNAN (2)

LEFT: Stone patio surfaces are durable, but extending the areas with gravel cuts costs.
ABOVE: Brick lining around the fish pond links it visually to the house; vines soften the brick walls.

siderate of your neighbors: Don't shine light in their windows.

For safety reasons, outdoor lighting fixtures should be sturdy and use a low-voltage light system. Look for shatterproof bulbs, too. All should have the UL label. Finally, consider dimmers to control the wattage of your scheme, and a timer to turn lights on and off when you're not there.

A PATIO FOR ALL SEASONS

In the improve-don't-move school, the couple who own the one-story brick ranch shown at left stand out as veterans. One of the first projects they tackled when they bought the house in Houston was the backyard. At the time, a chain-link fence separated their weed-choked lawn and pea-gravel patio from their neighbors' grounds. Their early-'80s makeover included a wooden deck, arbor, and hot tub. But by 1998 those amenities seemed out of date, and the arbor, now overgrown, made the patio feel closed in. The couple turned for advice to John S. Steele and David Samuelson, landscape architects with McDugald-Steele, a local firm. Together they planned and executed a complete redesign of the yard.

The scheme encompasses three distinct yet interrelated areas. Closest to the house is a 20-foot-square patio, the part the couple uses most. Paved in buckhorn charcoal flagstone and

banded in brick, the patio can be reached from the living room through new divided-light doors, as well as from the master bedroom and kitchen. Because the flagstones sit atop the old pea gravel, the patio is elevated 6 inches above the adjoining graveled seating area (main photo, previous page). The steps are single pieces of flagstone that frame the gravel. A 5-by-6-foot brick-walled fish pond marks the junction between the two sections; the pump that fed the old hot tub now circulates water in the pond.

To complement the design, Samuelson and Steele created a lush planting scheme that requires little maintenance. On one wall of the patio they strung a trellis of vinyl-coated cable, which hosts a thriving star jasmine, and planted maidenhair fern and leopard plant beneath to offset the flagstones. Shooting star (*Clerodendron*) and crape myrtle flank the doors into the living room.

A BUILT-IN OUTDOOR KITCHEN

Asked by his clients Gail and Smitty Smith to design a barbecue area behind their Los Angeles home, designer Nick Berman was faced with two major challenges: First, create a space that would be sensitive to the site—three acres of terraced vegetation woven throughout with stone paths. And second, choose materials that would be as beautiful as any selected for an indoor kitchen yet would stand up to the weather.

The Smiths had been happy with most of their

ABOVE: Teak cabinets are weather resistant. The true thickness of the granite countertops above them is visible around the sink. Thickened edges make the countertops seem far more massive than they really are.

MARK LOHMAN

landscaping, but there was one spot close to the house that was ugly and overgrown. To make the area more inviting, Smitty thought of creating a patio with a modest, built-in barbecue as an anniversary gift to his wife, but as the couple began discussing their needs with Berman, the project expanded in scope—into a full-fledged outdoor kitchen measuring roughly 200 square feet. "It became her birthday present, too," Smitty laughs.

Berman applied the same design principles to this cooking area (photos, above) that he would use in any kitchen. Here, the plan focuses on two parallel

set in a random pattern and mortared into place; it also sheathes the base of each counter in the cooking area.

Prior to construction of the counters, Berman ran plumbing and wiring to the outdoor kitchen area. Then he had a concrete foundation poured on three levels to follow the topography of the yard. The steel-reinforced concrete-block walls of each counter were built atop the foundation, then faced with stone.

The stainless-steel outdoor kitchen equipment and durable teak cabinets were installed along with a bank of durable stainless-steel drawers. "Stainless drawers," says Berman, "are beautiful and practical—as well as being watertight."

The support structure for the counters was constructed of marine plywood. The countertops themselves are flamed granite ¾ inch thick, but Berman had them edged to give the illusion that they are much thicker. The granite was coated with a penetrating sealer that prevents stains but maintains the natural appearance of the stone.

Of course, the heart of any kitchen is the cooking surface, and an outdoor kitchen is no different. As outdoor entertaining spaces have become more sophisticated, so too has the cooking equipment in them. Outdoor grill options abound, from the modest, space-saving hibachi and round-domed, even-heating charcoal/wood kettle to gas-powered wagon grills. The latest trend is built-in, full-service ranges with features such as griddles and woks. Traditional charcoal grills are still a popular choice, especially because they can burn woods such as mesquite and hickory chips—although some gas grills are equipped with smoke trays to hold these flavor-enhancing woods. A charcoal/wood grill should have multiple air vents in both the lid and charcoal pit to control heat flow and temperature, an opening in the bottom for easy ash removal, and a hood.

Many homeowners opt for grills fueled by natural or propane gas because they fire up faster and are easier to clean than grills that require charcoal. Some gas grills have multiple burners so that different foods can cook at varying times and temperatures. The largest boast up to 120,000 Btu of cooking power—enough to spit-roast two chickens and grill a surf-and-turf dinner for four at the same time. Before purchasing a grill big enough for a small restaurant, though, take an honest look at your cooking habits and and an even closer look at your budget. If a $50 hibachi will do the job for you, there's no point in spending upwards of $5,000 for the ultimate grill—the money you save will buy a lot of patio.

counters, each 31 inches high. One has a built-in grill and drawers for cooking and food prep. The other includes a sink and under-counter refrigerator. The counter steps up to 42 inches behind the work zone so that guests can sit on stools and kibitz with the cook. As a practical matter, though, this also hides cooking clutter from the other seating areas.

A new 20-by-30-foot dining patio lies 25 feet away across the lawn and is linked to the kitchen patio by a sinuous path. For visual continuity, Berman chose Bouquet Canyon stone for both patios and the path. The rough-textured rock is

ABOVE: Along with a swimming pool and a dining patio, the new, multilevel outdoor kitchen provides ample opportunities for congenial gatherings.

Landscaping With Water

With their abundance of life and soothing sounds, ponds provide tranquility—and a landscape focal point

THERE WAS A TIME WHEN A SWIMMING pool was the American backyard dream. But custom fish ponds have surged ahead as the landscape luxury of choice. "So many people are putting in water gardens," says Joe Kalbas, of Firestone Building Products, which makes the rubber lining that keeps water from leaking out of a pond, "that landscapers who used to do nothing but lawns are becoming pond specialists." Liner sales are growing briskly, Kalbas says, fed in part by the popular do-it-yourself kits that make small ponds possible for under $500, a particularly attractive figure given that large custom ponds can easily cost $25,000 or more.

Spending time next to a water garden offers peaceful respite from a hectic day. It's a joy to watch nature take its course—water lilies bloom, tadpoles come to life, fish multiply. And the gentle sounds of falling water cover traffic noise, says landscape architect John Geiger, who installs and maintains dozens of ponds for clients in Connecticut and New York. "It's amazing what happens when we turn off a waterfall for repairs," he says. "Suddenly, the yard goes dead."

ABOVE: A plastic-lined wood tub with a 2×6 cap is the structure beneath this rectilinear water garden.
RIGHT: This curvilinear pond is edged with overhanging flagstone for a natural look.

BUILDING A SIMPLE POND

When Rolf Nelson decided to build a lily pond (page 44) in his Texas backyard, he called on his friend Richard Koogle, of Lilypons Water Gardens. Though large ponds built on difficult sites often call for teams of special contractors, this pond would be modest in size as well as construction. Eventually, Nelson hoped, it would be the focal point of a new garden area, which he planned to link to the house with a stepping-stone path.

Choosing the location for a pond calls for care. It shouldn't be sited in a low place, where runoff from the property can foul the water or dislodge the liner. This one also had to be located in full sun, away from the shadow of the house and overhanging tree limbs—Nelson wanted water lilies in his pond. This also eliminated the need to dig around tree roots and would reduce

BRIAN SMITH (4)

maintenance chores later on—Nelson didn't want to spend a lot of time dredging soggy clumps of leaves out of the water. It's also not a good idea to install a lined pond where the water table is high or the soil drains very poorly—hydrostatic pressure might actually lift the liner.

Once Nelson settled on a general location, the men plotted the shape of the pond by looping garden hose in various loose oval shapes until they found one they liked (top photo, opposite). Using the hose as a guide, they cut through the sod with a spade, then excavated the area with shovels. (If the soil is rocky, though, or the excavation large, rented power equipment saves a lot of time at this stage.) Rather than hauling the dirt away—more work—the men simply piled it on one side of the pond to form a small berm that might someday be planted. As the excavation neared an end, the grade was evened out around the edges by scrap-

This Texas water garden captures the sky and reflects its light back to the landscape. The modest pond would later become the focal point of a patio and the inspiration for further plantings.

ing down high areas and building up low ones. Progress was checked with a level taped to a straight 2×4 (middle photo, opposite).

The hole for a pond should be dug with a flat bottom and gently sloping sides. Experts recommend ringing it with 12-inch-deep shelves on which to set potted shallow-water plants, and digging the rest of the area down at least 18 inches for water lilies. Matting around the sides of the excavation and a layer of sand on the bottom are precautions often taken to keep any remaining sharp stones and roots from damaging the liner. In this case, a synthetic feltlike underlayment fabric was cut into panels to fit the sides.

In keeping with the naturalistic shape of the pond, Nelson and Koogle decided not to make a formal necklace of coping stones around the rim. Instead, they decided to set stones only on the north side, closest to the house. Using local stone and making the edge somewhat irregular avoided the look of a pool just plunked into the landscape. After digging a shallow trench so the tops of the stones were roughly at grade level, Koogle installed steel lawn edging around the rest of the excavation to support the liner on that side. The liner went under the rocks on one side and over the edging on the other, where it was trimmed off 4 inches beyond the rim with a utility knife, and then buried beneath sod.

With a pond, inspiration always leads to excavation. Here, the pond is designed with garden hose (TOP), then excavated (MIDDLE). Edges must be even to prevent the liner from showing. With the liner in place (BOTTOM), the bottom was covered with a protective layer of sand.

Liners come in many sizes and are made from materials such as inexpensive PVC or more expensive, longer-lasting rubber. Thicker liners last longer—up to 50 years. When it came time to install the unwieldy liner, it was folded into a strip and carried to the hole, then unfolded and allowed to settle (bottom photo, left). Creases were smoothed out wherever possible, but the weight of water pressing against the liner would minimize the appearance of any that remained.

With the liner in place, Nelson and Koogle set the stone in mortar, arranging it with a 3-inch overhang that casts a shadow on the water—that makes the pond look deeper and gives it a natural look. When the excess liner was trimmed, they shoveled soil against the backside of the stone to complete construction. The first fill water was made dirty and alkaline by the mortar, so it had to be siphoned out and the pond refilled.

PLANTS AND FISH FOR PONDS

In keeping with the modest proportions of his pond, Nelson stocked it simply. He placed water lilies on the pond floor and shallow-water plants on the shelves. But some homeowners spare no effort to build and stock their pond.

Twenty years ago, a businessman and his wife were bewitched by a particular waterfront property in Connecticut. What attracted them was not the house, a '50s ranch, but the land on which it sits: two acres of lawn and rock outcrop that slope steadily down to a broad expanse of exposed rock ledge and Long Island Sound. Hoping to make the most of the site, the pair called John Geiger & Associates, a Redding, Connecticut, landscape design firm. Landscape architect Liz Hand-Fry took one look at the site and knew it would great for a waterscape (photos, following pages).

Once the waterfall's hardscaping and systems were in place, it was time for Mark Krasnickas to bring life to the ponds. First up: conditioning the chlorinated fill water in the pools with a neutralizer to stabilize ammonia levels and make the environment safe for fish. Next came the flora. To create a planting bed around the ponds' stone borders, he trucked in 60 yards of topsoil. Grasses were one of the many plants—sedum, thyme, Russian sage, yarrow, and heather are others—chosen by Hand-Fry for their visual variety and ability to stand up to the wind, sun, and salt air.

The pond bottoms are covered with a rubber liner, so nothing can be planted directly in soil. Instead, Krasnickas set potted plants—including iris, pickerel rush, lotus, horsetail, and water lilies, stacking bricks on the pond floor so he could set

ABOVE: Concrete block forms the walls of the large lower pond. To form the floor, concrete was poured directly on the exposed bedrock. Six yards of top-soil were then dumped in and shaped into gentle, natural-looking curves to support a rubber liner.
RIGHT: The nearly-complete installation.

flowers above the water. Then he topped off each plant's soil with pea stone.

Krasnickas floated water hyacinths in both ponds. These fragile tropical plants extract nourishment from the water via their dangling roots. To ensure that those in the upper pond wouldn't wash over the falls, he secured them with thin wire to stones at the pond's base.

Koi, or ornamental carp, completed the tableau. These hardy specimens can reach three feet in length, live 50 to 70 years, and winter over in a pond as long as moving water keeps the surface from freezing. They can be expensive, but Hand-Fry believes they're worth their average price of $100 to $500 for a 10-inch fish. With distinctive coloration and individual personalities, "they become pets," she says. The nine koi released live amicably alongside bright red-orange-and-white comets, and blue-, orange-, and red-spotted shubunkin.

To acclimate the fish for release into the pond, Krasnickas floated them in plastic bags filled with water for half an hour. Then he opened the bags, exchanged a third of the water for pond water, resealed the bags, and let them bob another 20 minutes. After repeating that step a second time, Krasnickas released each swimmer into its new eden.

KOLIN SMITH (4)

ABOVE: During a test run of the waterfall, workers shifted stones to fine-tune the water flow.

BELOW: When the water was ready, a mix of koi and other fish were introduced after a careful process of acclimating them to conditions. The newcomer being released here is a comet.

Small-Space Landscaping

Here are some ways to make a small yard, or an oddly shaped section of a large one, look and feel bigger

Turning a small space into a garden is a lot like furnishing a studio apartment. The challenge is making the most of the space you have and, often, creating space where you thought you had none.

Whether your small garden is a 50×50-ft. plot, a narrow side yard, the length of a patio or deck, or an oddly shaped pocket of ground, various techniques will help you make that area seem bigger. Plus, they'll help you turn it into an inviting, useful space for people, as well as for plants.

CREATE A UNIFIED THEME

A random collection of plants and landscaping materials can make small spaces feel cluttered and confining because the details of each plant and surface tend to stand out. For example, an ailing shrub with yellowing leaves may go unnoticed in a large garden. But in a small space such an eyesore makes the entire garden look unhealthy. That same phenomenon works in reverse: A single pot of vibrant tulips can transform a dull corner into an inviting oasis. Other strategies to consider:

• Keep things simple. Stick to one look so each garden element becomes an integral part of the whole. Eliminate details that don't contribute to the function or look of the garden.

• Start with a plan for the entire space even if you don't do all the work at once. This helps avoid a piecemeal look.

• Choose a few plants that work together and use them repeatedly through the garden.

• Repeat colors and construction materials to help tie everything together.

REPLACE LAWN WITH PAVING

Most homeowners plant grass in open areas. But corner-to-corner lawn in a small space looks ugly and isn't functional. Brick, stone, or wood paving usually is a better choice. Paving looks good, reduces maintenance, and makes the space more useful.

Paving accommodates everything from tricycles and built-in

ABOVE: This pocket-sized patio provides seclusion and a place to relax in an urban front yard.
RIGHT: Container plants, patio furniture, and sculpture accent a rustic backyard patio enclosed by a rose-clad fence.

SAXON HOLT (2)

planters to furniture. To determine how much hard surface you need, keep the following in mind:

- A tricycle can stay on a 24-inch walk and turn in a 4- to 6-foot circle.

- An eating area for eight requires at least 144 square feet. You'll also need an 8×6-foot space for the barbecue—and the chef.

- Before paving a surface, lay out boundaries with a garden hose or rope to help you visualize the space. Test the area by putting furniture or people into the outlined zone.

If your garden is next to the house, make the two work together by choosing paving that repeats some of the colors and building materials of your home. Paving often looks best when softened by plants, whether they spill over the edges or grow densely between stones. Paving materials that are small and fine, rather than large and coarse, are least likely to overpower small spaces. Brick is a great choice. It comes in a variety of sizes and colors, and it can be laid in many interesting patterns.

Wood decking is another popular option. Laying boards horizontally makes a narrow garden appear wider, while orienting them lengthwise adds depth to a wide, shallow garden.

PUT WALLS TO WORK
Undesirable views and lack of privacy are typical problems walls help solve. Unfortunately, high walls in a small space can feel claustrophobic. For a more open feeling, attach lattice on top of a concrete-block wall or solid wood fence. You can also make a wall seem less forboding by making a small window to a pleasant view.

Before adding on to walls or fences, check local ordinances for the maximum allowable height and locations. Also be cautious about vines: Clinging ones, such as English ivy and Virginia creeper, are so tenacious that removing them later will damage painted or plastered surfaces, and it's hard to paint a vine-covered wall. As an alternative, you might want to consider building a trellis a few feet from the wall to support clinging vines.

PICK PLANTS THAT FIT
When choosing plants for small spaces, be sure they won't grow too large for the space. That way, you'll avoid the hassle of constant pruning or eventually having to remove plants when they overwhelm the area.

- Small trees that grow 10 to 30 feet high are perfect candidates for small yards. Among them are purple-leaf plum, vine maple, mayten tree, palo verde, Japanese maple, serviceberry, silver bell, Eastern redbud, and flowering dogwood.

SAXON HOLT

Potted rose and orange-red lillies accent a terraced patio. The teak bench was discreetly tucked into a private niche.

- If a standard tree won't fit comfortably, consider planting a dwarf variety. A dwarf apple tree, for example, grows only 6 to 10 feet high.

- Also consider large shrubs like pineapple guava or xylosma, which can be trained to look like a multi-trunked tree.

- In narrow spaces like side yards, choose plants that grow up, not out. Vines are the obvious choice, though shrubs such as heavenly bamboo, twisted juniper, and yew pine are easy to keep narrow.

When choosing container plants, don't rely solely on flowering annuals. They look good for one summer, then you have to start all over again. If you choose them carefully, shrubs and trees provide a year-round show with their shapes, turning leaves, flowers, berries, and interesting bark. You can also grow fruits and vegetables in containers. A single bush or patio tomato planted in a bushel basket yields pounds of fruit.

• Make sure each container drains well; otherwise roots will become waterlogged and suffocate.

• Use a fast-draining potting soil or a soilless mix; ordinary garden soil is too dense and retains too much moisture for most container plants.

• Support large containers on bricks and place saucers beneath small containers. This prevents the water that seeps out of drainage holes from staining your deck or paving.

Also remember that containers don't allow roots to wander in search of food and water. You'll have to provide these essentials regularly during the growing season.

STRETCH YOUR BOUNDARIES

Making a tight space feel roomy is largely a matter of fooling the eye. Using focal points such as a large container plant or small fountain is one such trick. Focal points hold your attention in a garden and keep you from immediately seeing abrupt boundaries. In the same way, plants growing overhead on an arbor draw your eye upward.

Another way to counter close-in boundaries is to blur them with plants. Grouping a few different kinds of plants with varying sizes, shapes and textures creates a sense of depth, and that makes the garden feel more spacious. Color also creates the illusion of depth. Cool colors, such as blue and violet, tend to recede. Placed at the farthest edge of a garden, they give an impression of distance. Because warm colors, such as yellow and orange, seem to jump forward, place them sparingly in a small area.

If a beautiful view lies beyond your property line, extend your boundaries by framing the scene and incorporating it into your garden. Selectively prune trees to open a visual window to the view. Or, in an open space, use a rose-covered arching trellis to capture it.

Changing levels in a garden, or lengthening the route through it, can also make the area feel larger. Just a few steps down to a pond or up to a raised deck can make a short path more interesting. Likewise, a gently curving path gives an illusion of distance compared with a straight one. And when the path leads out of view or ends at a door or gate, it suggests that more garden lies beyond.

USE POTS, BARRELS, AND BASKETS

If your small area doesn't have much planting space or if the soil is poor, do your growing in containers. This practical alternative to growing in the ground brings color and life to an otherwise barren spot. You can cluster container-grown plants to create a dense tangle of growth or use them sparingly as accents. You can also suspend baskets from rafters, attach pots to walls, or give added emphasis to a container plant by featuring it on a raised surface, such as a low wall or pedestal.

Solving Site Problems

Before other work starts, correct poor drainage and use retaining walls to sculpt awkward slopes

STABBING THE GROUND WITH HIS SHOVEL, DOMINICK Rattacasa tries to start a hole. The shovel barely breaks the surface, its blade no match for the dense, glacial soil prevalent in the area. Besides being tough to dig in, dirt like this doesn't soak up much rainwater. Instead of percolating into the ground, water obeys gravity and heads downhill—in this case straight for the house.

When it gets there, says Rattacasa, an excavation and landscape contractor, the basement turns into a reflecting pool. In heavy downpours, so much water speeds down the slope that little waves slap against the house, leaving muddy marks on the pale-yellow stucco and turning the yard into a swamp. The lawn ponds frequently, he says. "Hardly anything grows at all."

A lawn that squishes underfoot spells doom for plants, says Jud Griggs, president of the Associated Landscape Contractors of America. "When roots get saturated, they lose oxygen, and plants suffocate." Signs of trouble include stunted growth and wilted or black-edged foliage, he adds. Saturated ground also breeds unsightly molds and fungi and, where water collects in shallow pools, mosquitoes.

Yet despite the damage poor drainage can inflict, fixing it doesn't rank high among homeowners' landscaping priorities. "Humans are incredibly adaptable," says Tom Dunbar, president of the American Society of Landscape Architects. "A lot of people just ignore the water. They simply give up that part of their yard." Contractors say that clients are often reluctant to sink money into something they can't see. But without better drainage, there will be little to admire in any backyard.

To change the course of all that water, Rattacasa brought in a small squadron of earthmovers—an excavator, backhoe, bulldozer, skid loader, and dump truck—along with 160 yards of drainage stone, hundreds of feet of 4-inch perforated pipe, and a blueprint of the new drainage system. It was developed by Charles J. Stick, a landscape architect who had already designed the parklike front yard, dotting it with trees and shrubs indigenous to the region. His plan for the backyard included patios, pathways, planting beds, and dozens of trees, none of which can go in until the ground gets a lot drier.

Stick's drainage system consists of subsurface water movers, called French drains. These horizontal trenches intercept water

KOLIN SMITH (3)

ABOVE LEFT: Lining trenches with landscaping fabric keeps silt out of pipes. LEFT: Perforated drainage pipe.

flowing down a slope, then drain it to a more convenient location. A typical drain begins as a 3-foot-deep trench lined with fiberglass landscaping fabric to keep out silt that could ultimately clog the drainpipe. After dumping in about 4 inches of drainage stone, Rattacasa's crew lays in 10-foot sections of perforated drainpipe, glues them together, and covers them with more drainage stone. On top goes a 6-inch layer of topsoil, a drainage-friendly replacement for the hard-as-a-rock dirt that often comes from the trenches.

To collect as much surface water as possible, the uppermost trench at this project was filled entirely with drainage stone, with no soil or sod on top. "Because there is so little percolation," says Stick, "an open trench like this is the most effective way to intercept water." Eventually, English ivy and a hedge will grow to hide the stone. Each run of perforated pipe ends at an unperforated 6-inch collection pipe leading to "daylight."

Water that gets by this gauntlet of drains will be caught in a swale, a shallow channel that Rattacasa's backhoe carved between the house and the base of the slope. The swale has plumbing, too: a string of three surface drains, flush with the sod, linked by 4-inch solid pipe buried just 6 inches below. The swale will also fix a common yard defect: poor grading, a condition usually created when a site is first cleared. "Regardless of whether a house is new or 100 years old, the yard is usually a result of how the builders left it," says Dunbar. Builders and owners alike put off or altogether avoid hiring a landscaper to shape the ground. But most problems can be corrected by regrading to create the right amount of slope, adding dirt to fill sinkholes, or cutting a swale to reroute runoff. Sometimes, getting control of the flow requires reshaping the land entirely. The 10 feet of ground closest to the house should slope at least 6 inches downward, says Griggs, to keep water from seeping into the basement or flooding foundation plantings. Lawns require less of a grade: at least 1 inch of slope for every 5 feet of turf.

The general idea, says Rattacasa, is simple: "We're trying to get the water before it gets to the house." This land is wetter than most. "The builder hit so much water when he dug the foundation that he had to bring in 3,000 yards of dirt to raise the house." Low in organic matter, some of the fill was spread across the yard and compacted by heavy machinery. To make the ground more porous, Stick has prescribed annual treatments with an aerator, which will pull out dirt plugs and replace them with pelletized gypsum and humus.

Once the drain system is installed, the real test will be the spring rains. If runoff overwhelms 600 feet of French drain, Rattacasa can add even more drainage. Leaving nothing to chance, Stick's plan includes vertical pipes—now capped just below the surface—that tie into the perforated pipe. To catch more rainwater and snowmelt, the verticals can be connected to the same kind of surface drains used in the swale. "This way, we know we'll have the drainage we need," says Stick. "It means the difference between having a garden and not having a garden."

RETAINING WALLS

Soggy soil can make an uncooperative site, but so too can slopes that pitch awkwardly or erode bit by bit whenever it rains. Sculpting the site with retaining walls is one fix. These walls are carefully engineered systems that wage an ongoing battle with gravity. They restrain tons of saturated soil that would otherwise slump and slide away. Along with solving erosion problems, retaining walls can also eliminate slopes too difficult—or dangerous—to mow. They're also used where the downhill side of a foundation is losing supporting soil or its uphill side is under pressure from sliding soil. Unfortunately, many such walls aren't able to handle the hillside they're supposed to hold back.

Even small retaining walls have to contain enormous loads. A 4-foot-high, 15-foot-long wall could be holding back as much as 20 tons of saturated soil. Double the wall height to 8 feet, and you would need a wall that's eight times stronger to do the same job. With forces like these in play, you should limit your retaining wall efforts to under 4 feet tall (3 feet for mortarless stone). If you need a taller wall, consider step-terracing the lot with two walls half as big, or call in a landscape architect or structural engineer for the design work (have one or the other inspect the site thoroughly). Rely on an experienced builder for the installation.

Four types of retaining walls are commonly used for residential applications:

• Timber walls. Assembled from 6×6 preservative-treated lumber (drawing, above), timber walls are inexpensive and relatively easy to build. Wood should be designated For Ground Contact. Timber isn't as durable as masonry.

• Interlocking concrete block. These systems consist of small, easy to assemble masonry units that lock together in various ways without mortar. Many textures, shapes, and colors are avail-

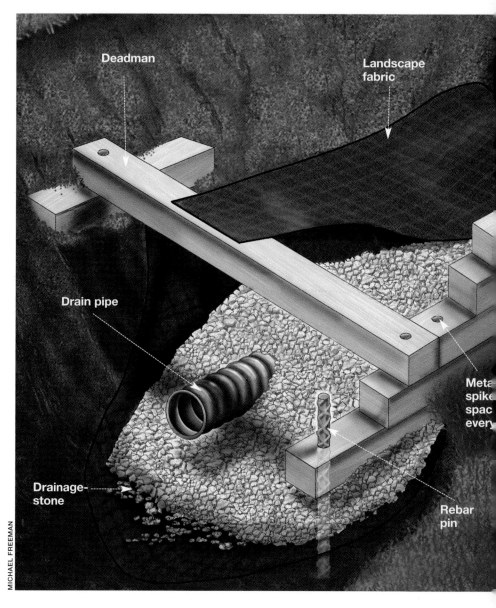

Deadman

Landscape fabric

Drain pipe

Drainage-stone

Meta spike spac every

Rebar pin

MICHAEL FREEMAN

able, and the systems can make straight walls or walls that curve and taper.

• Stone. Nothing beats wall stone (photo, opposite) for handsome, rustic appeal. Walls can be dry-fit or laid up with mortar, but fitting wall stone is exacting work.

• Concrete and concrete block. When reinforced with steel, these make the strongest walls, though they aren't particularly attractive unless faced with another material, such as stone veneer. Leave these walls to the pros.

Like most outdoor structures, retaining walls need a solid foundation for durability. Mortared or concrete walls in heavy-frost areas require footings dug below the frost line. If you live where it doesn't freeze and your soil drains well, you may be able to just scrape away the topsoil to form a base for nonmortared walls.

CRAIG RAINE

As a retaining wall rises, it should be backfilled to encourage drainage. Drainage stone (not gravel) is the usual backfill material, but first, lay down enough landscape fabric to contain it (drawing, above left). You'll need enough fabric to be able to form a large C shape, with the open portion facing downhill. The fabric separates the drainage stone and topsoil to keep sediment from clogging the stone and the drainpipe.

Backfill should be uniformly graded (all one size) washed stone ranging from ¾ inch to 6 inch in diameter. Shovel at least a 4-inch layer onto the landscape fabric. Grade this layer to drain water away; it should slope 1 inch for every 4 feet of run. Then lay in 4-inch perforated PVC drainpipe and cover it with another layer of stone.

Don't add backfill all at once because it won't compact thoroughly. Instead, add it as

By creating flat terraces, retaining walls transform awkward slopes into usable space that's often easier to maintain. The walls here are dry-laid stone.

you build the wall, and tamp it down as you go. After folding landscape fabric over the last layer of stone, add 6 inches of topsoil and lightly compact it.

All retaining walls should lean into the hill 1 inch for every foot of height. Timber walls 4 feet or higher should be tied to the hillside with "deadman" anchors (T-shaped tiebacks buried in the hillside) attached to the wall every 8 feet. They typically extend 6 feet back into the hillside, and terminate at a 2-foot long T-bar. Other types of deadman anchors may be required with some types of interlocking block systems. Each system is different, however, so be sure to check installation details with the manufacturer.

One other thing: Any tree growing within 4 feet or so, depending on its root structure, can eventually destroy even the best-made wall.

Trees, Sh

rubs & Vines

PROBLEM-SOLVING CHOICES FOR YOUR YARD

Whatever goals you may have for introducing decks, walks, and other "hardscaping" elements to your yard, a well balanced-landscape plan always calls for something that grows. Whether you prefer the exuberant behavior of a climbing rose or the spare sculpture of a privet hedge, you'll find an abundance of ideas in the following pages for making thoughtful choices—and you'll learn how to make the best use of them.

Flowering Trees

Choose a native species to show-off in your landscape

EACH SPRING, PAT STONE'S YARD EXPLODES WITH color as a dozen trees begin to bloom. Though she planted them as young trees, each could have appeared naturally in this part of western North Carolina, for they all are indigenous to the area. Similar scenes unfold in nearly any area of the country, wherever indigenous species are encouraged.

Native trees make excellent choices in most any landscape because they are well adapted to their local climates, and many bring unique characteristics and startling beauty to the scenery. In the Southwest, for instance, the bark of a blue paloverde actually photosynthesizes, making it as green as the leaves. A profusion of fluffy plumes give a cloudlike appearance to the fringe tree—native from Pennsylvania to Texas. And the gentle white blooms that dangle from a Carolina silver bell in spring become four-winged green fruits in fall.

Sure, garden centers sell truckloads of European and Asian ornamentals hybridized for hardiness and showy flowers. But in an era when quaint Main Streets give way to cookie-cutter malls and most garden catalogs offer the same standard options, growing native trees helps, in a small way, to protect the botanical diversity of this vast continent. The sampling of natives shown on these pages represents natural ranges large and small, and are available from good regional nurseries.

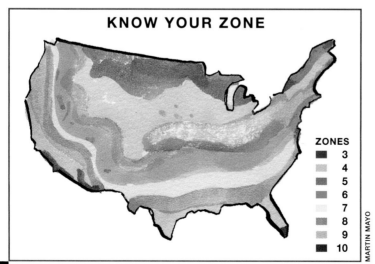

KNOW YOUR ZONE

ZONES
- 3
- 4
- 5
- 6
- 7
- 8
- 9
- 10

MARTIN MAYO

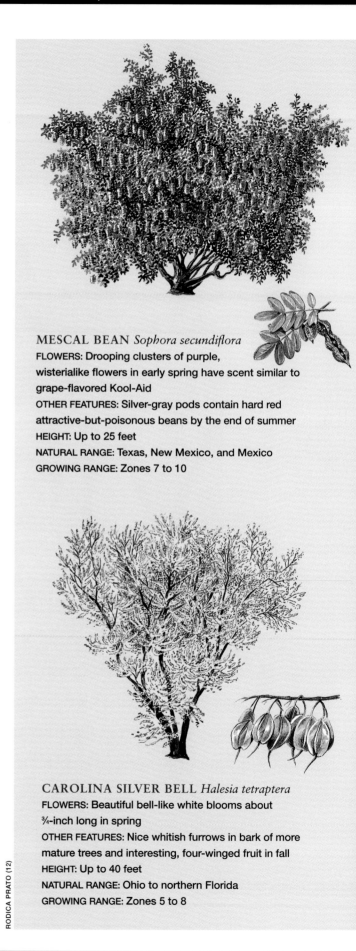

RODICA PRATO (12)

MESCAL BEAN *Sophora secundiflora*
FLOWERS: Drooping clusters of purple, wisterialike flowers in early spring have scent similar to grape-flavored Kool-Aid
OTHER FEATURES: Silver-gray pods contain hard red attractive-but-poisonous beans by the end of summer
HEIGHT: Up to 25 feet
NATURAL RANGE: Texas, New Mexico, and Mexico
GROWING RANGE: Zones 7 to 10

CAROLINA SILVER BELL *Halesia tetraptera*
FLOWERS: Beautiful bell-like white blooms about ¾-inch long in spring
OTHER FEATURES: Nice whitish furrows in bark of more mature trees and interesting, four-winged fruit in fall
HEIGHT: Up to 40 feet
NATURAL RANGE: Ohio to northern Florida
GROWING RANGE: Zones 5 to 8

DOWNY SERVICEBERRY *Amelanchier arborea*
FLOWERS: Tufts of white flowers in early spring,
just before leaves emerge
OTHER FEATURES: Small multistemmed or single-trunked tree
produces attractive red-purple berries in June that are loved by
birds and are good for jam
HEIGHT: Up to 25 feet
NATURAL RANGE: Eastern Canada to Georgia
GROWING RANGE: Zones 4 to 9

DESERT WILLOW *Chilopsis linearis*
FLOWERS: Rose-pink to purple trumpet-shaped
flowers bloom from midspring into summer
OTHER FEATURES: Flowers attract humingbirds;
tree has an interesting twisted trunk
HEIGHT: Up to 25 feet
NATURAL RANGE: Desert regions from Texas to California and Mexico
GROWING RANGE: Zones 7 to 10

FRANKLINIA *Franklinia alatamaha*
FLOWERS: Solitary camellialike 3-inch flowers
with yellow centers beginning in late July to August
OTHER FEATURES: Leaves turn red and burgundy in fall
HEIGHT: Up to 30 feet
NATURAL RANGE: Banks of the Altamaha River in Georgia
GROWING RANGE: Zones 5 to 9

MADRONA *Arbutus menziesii*
FLOWERS: Showy clusters of small white honey-scented blooms in spring
OTHER FEATURES: Dark, glossy evergreen leaves; smooth
cinnamon-red bark that peels off between June and September
HEIGHT: Up to 30 feet
NATURAL RANGE: Western British Columbia to San Francisco and Sierra
Nevada in California
GROWING RANGE: Zones 7 to 10

Consult a zone map (drawing, page 58) to get a idea of where else these trees will thrive.

PLANTING A BARE-ROOT TREE

"Never put a $20 tree in a 50-cent hole." That saying taught generations of landscapers that the proper way to give trees a healthy start was to dig a crater twice the size of the root ball, shovel in fertilizer, and build a water-holding trough around the transplant. But current horticultural research has challenged the benefits of those steps, a fact that Robert Kourik, a California landscape designer and author of *The Tree and Shrub Finder*, had to see to believe. "I'd read all the reports, but I was skeptical," he says. "Then I noticed that the trees with the most soil amendments were the most likely to blow over. I investigated, and found that all their roots were still in the planting hole!"

It turns out that if the soil in the hole is looser and richer than the surrounding earth, when the roots hit the edge of the hole, they'll circle back for the easier nutrient source. But roots must spread out. "People think roots grow down. But most grow shallow and wide—as much as three times farther than the branches—and make the tree stable," says Kourik. Spreading roots help the tree survive droughts, too, by casting a wider net for groundwater.

So Kourik changed his approach to planting bare-root trees, sold dormant in later winter or early spring (see page 62 for information about planting container trees). Using a digging fork, he makes his hole no wider than the root ball and just deep enough to remove sod and weed roots. He pokes the fork into the sides and bottom of the hole to loosen the surrounding earth, and then builds a mound inside the hole that rises 6 to 8 inches above grade and slopes to the bottom of the hole. After shaking off the soil on the roots and fanning them over the mound, Kourik covers them with 2 to 6 inches of earth. Mulch forms a 2- to 4-inch layer over that soil but shouldn't come within 6 inches of the trunk itself—that would encourage rot. He supports the tree with two stakes shorter than the lowest branches, with rubber straps to hold the tree in position without damaging the limbs. The straps are available at nurseries.

For the tree's first watering, Kourik soaks the mound heavily, but from then on he only waters underneath the ends of the branches, encouraging the tree's roots to reach out for moisture. "The wider the roots grow, the less dependent they'll be on your care," he says.

HAWTHORN *Crataegus*
FLOWERS: Profuse small white flowers in mid- to late spring
OTHER FEATURES: Lovely small orange-red fruit appears in the fall and hangs on into winter
HEIGHT: Up to 30 feet
NATURAL RANGE: Dozens of hawthorn varieties are native to an area extending from New England to South Carolina to Indiana
GROWING RANGE: Zones 4 to 8

RED BUCKEYE *Aesculus pavia*
FLOWERS: 3- to 6-inch-long clusters of drooping coral-red flowers in late summer
OTHER FEATURES: Attractive orange-brown nuts (inedible) in October; leaves are toxic to deer, brown seeds look like eye of a buck
HEIGHT: Up to 25 feet
NATURAL RANGE: Virginia to Florida, and Louisiana to Texas
GROWING RANGE: Zones 4 to 8

RODICA PRATO (12)

COMMON WITCH HAZEL *Hamamelis virginiana*
FLOWERS: Spidery yellow flowers bloom in autumn or winter, before or after leaves have fallen
OTHER FEATURES: Leaves turn gold in fall; seed pods explode, propelling seeds away; trunks tend to develop multiple stems
HEIGHT: Up to 30 feet
NATURAL RANGE: Nova Scotia to Florida and Texas and Iowa
GROWING RANGE: Zones 3 to 8

FELTLEAF CEANOTHUS *Ceanothus arboreus*
FLOWERS: Showy, fragrant deep-blue to pale-lavender flowers in large 4- to 6-inch clusters in spring
OTHER FEATURES: Evergreen leaves, glossy on top, whitish underneath
HEIGHT: Up to 25 feet
NATURAL RANGE: Catalina Island, California
GROWING RANGE: Zones 8 to 10

FRINGE TREE *Chionanthus virginicus*
FLOWERS: Fragrant white flowers in 4- to 8-inch-long clusters bloom in late spring
OTHER FEATURES: Abundant dark-blue fruit ripens on female trees in late summer or early fall if there's a male tree in the area
HEIGHT: Up to 35 feet; has tendency to sprout several shrublike trunks
NATURAL RANGE: Eastern U.S. from Pennsylvania to Texas
GROWING RANGE: Zones 4 to 9

BLUE PALOVERDE *Cercidium floridum*
FLOWERS: Masses of striking bright-yellow flowers in late spring
OTHER FEATURES: Green bark actually photosynthesizes; tree will drop leaves in extreme heat or cold
HEIGHT: Up to 25 feet
NATURAL RANGE: Southwest, particularly Arizona and New Mexico
GROWING RANGE: Zones 8 to 10

Putting Down Roots

How to plant a tree in your yard— and care for it afterwards

THERE'S NOTHING YOU CAN ADD TO YOUR YARD THAT improves it as much as a tree does. As a practical matter, a tree can provide shade, block harsh winds, and even muffle the noise of a busy street. It can even add value to your home. But looks count, too, and a tree is a continual source of beauty as it grows over the years and changes throughout the seasons.

It's not difficult to make the most of a tree's potential—if you're armed with a little knowledge about choosing the best site in your yard, buying the right stock, and planting it correctly. "The worst thing," says Roger Cook, "is to plant a tree too low—its roots will suffocate and the tree will die."

LOCATING A TREE

If you know where you want to plant a tree, then you need to look for a species that you like, that will grow well in the soil and sun at the site, and that won't outgrow the location over its lifetime. Finding a tree that will flourish in your yard is fairly simple—nurseries and the local extension service will provide you with a list of appropriate trees. But you still have to consider a tree's size and habits. For example, large shade trees, such as European beech or white oak, are great at bringing relief from summer heat. They shouldn't, however, be planted next to a swimming pool, where they'll create extra work for you by dropping their leaves into the water.

Other considerations include the tree's root system (surface roots can wreck a lawn and even lift concrete), maintenance needs (some trees require lots of pruning, others make you rake), and resistance to insects and disease.

As you look at different trees, you may change your mind on where you want to plant. Keep these other considerations in mind before you start digging:

• Don't plant close to the house. Plant a tree that spreads 40 feet wide at least 20 feet from the house.

• Avoid planting a tree where it will overhang your house, block a door, or obstruct a desirable view from indoors.

• Don't plant a tree beneath power lines if it will exceed a height of 25 feet

• Don't dig above underground utility lines. For help in locating electric, cable, phone, and waterlines on your property, contact each of your utility companies directly.

SAXON HOLT (3)

STEP 1: Begin by digging a hole as deep as the root ball and two to four times its width. (In heavy clay soil, make the hole 1 to 2 inches shallower than the root ball.) Widen the hole near the soil surface; then dig around the bottom of the hole to create a pedestal of undug soil. The solid pedestal supports the tree at the proper depth and keeps it from settling.

STEP 2: Remove the tree from its container and brush the soil off the outer few inches of the root ball. Cut off any circling roots on the outside of the root ball close to the tree base. Tease or pry apart matted roots to encourage them to grow outward. For a balled-and-burlapped tree, remove the pinning nails, wire basket, rope, and synthetic or treated burlap (leave natural burlap in place).

This well-planted tree with a balanced branch structure does not require staking, but regular watering after planting is essential.

• Plant where roots have ample room to grow. Be cautious near sewer and drain lines (roots can puncture them), paved surfaces (they will buckle), and even areas of lawn (surface roots steal water and make mowing a nightmare).

• Consider visibility. Position a tree with low-growing branches far from the corner of a block so it won't block the vision of motorists who stop at the intersection.

• Be a good neighbor. Don't plant a tree directly on or near your property line.

THE RIGHT TREE

A tree is a lifetime investment, so don't buy strictly on price. And put some thought into where

SAXON HOLT (4)

3

you buy. Staff members at a quality nursery or garden center know trees, sell the best varieties, and offer information and assistance you may not get elsewhere. They will know what soil and sun conditions each species requires, how tall it will grow, and can describe its flowers and leaves in each season for any tree they sell. The trees they have on hand should be robust and in good health; also make sure they're labeled with their common and botanical names—and the price.

Most nurseries also provide valuable services. Many guarantee the health of a tree for a year. Delivery is usually available for an extra charge, and some nurseries will even plant the tree for you, as long as you arrange this ahead of time.

Trees are sold two ways in early summer, the time when many people start their shopping: balled-and-burlapped (often abbreviated as B&B by nurseries) and, most commonly, in containers. A balled-and-burlapped tree is dug from a nursery

STEP 3: Set the tree in the hole on the pedestal. Roll back any burlap that's still in place and trim away as much as you can. Backfill the hole halfway with soil excavated from the hole. Don't mix organic matter such as peat moss into the backfill soil: Changing the soil texture in a planting hole inhibits water movement as well as root growth into surrounding soil.

field with a ball of soil around the roots, and the ball is wrapped in burlap and tied. A tree in a container might have been grown in that container or transplanted from a nursery field into the pot when close to sellable size.

Although prices are comparable, a tree in a container with a soilless growing medium (usually sand and bark) weighs less and is easier to handle than a balled-and-burlapped tree, which typically weighs 100 pounds per cubic foot of root ball.

Regardless of how the tree was grown, bigger is not always better. Research shows that a smaller tree suffers less transplant stress and grows more quickly after transplanting than a larger one. What's more, a smaller tree costs less and is easier to maneuver. But it takes time for a small tree to catch up to a larger one. Your choice comes down to the immediate gratification of a large tree versus the cost, vigor, and convenience of a small tree.

Make sure the tree is healthy. Select a tree with

STEP 4: Water the soil in the partially filled hole thoroughly. This rehydrates the soil and root ball, and settles out air pockets that can cause roots to dry out.

evenly spaced branches extending in all directions. The leaves should be even colored and free of insects and disease. Reject any tree with broken branches, wounds circling the trunk, or sap oozing from it.

The root ball should feel moist. Even one or two missed waterings at the nursery can harm a tree. It's also important to check the root system of plants in containers. Circling or kinked roots on the root ball surface indicate serious problems; circling roots can strangle the tree years later.

Ideally, a tree should be able to stand on its own without being tightly staked. Ask a nursery staff member to untie a staked tree you're interested in; if the tree then bends at a sharp angle away from the stake, don't buy it.

Once you've purchased your tree, protect it on the trip home. Lift and carry it from underneath the root ball or container, not by the trunk. If the tree is being transported in the open air, wrap its top in burlap or a similar material. This protects the plant from wind that can break branches or shred and dehydrate the leaves.

FOLLOW-UP CARE

Keep the soil moist around a newly planted tree, not soaking wet. The root ball could dry out in a day or two, especially in hot summer weather. Once established, a tree needs about 1 inch of water a week over the root zone through the growing season, whether from rainfall or irrigation.

Spread a 2- to 3-inch-thick layer of mulch at the base of the tree, keeping it away from the trunk. Mulch conserves moisture, protects against temperature extremes, and reduces competition from weeds. It also prevents your lawn mower from grazing the trunk and damaging it.

STEP 5: Finish backfilling the hole. Don't cover the top of the root ball with soil because this can prevent water from reaching the roots.

STEP 6: Finish off by spreading mulch at the base of the tree, keeping it away from the trunk.

Stake the tree only if necessary; a tree establishes more quickly and is stronger if it's not staked. Only a top-heavy tree or one on a windy site should be staked to prevent it from toppling over. Secure the tree with plastic or nylon strapping to protect the bark—wire sheathed with garden hose damages trees. Also, allow the tree a slight amount of flex, rather than holding it rigidly in place. Remove all staking materials after one year to prevent them from girdling the trunk.

Take good care of your young tree and it will pay you back many times over, sooner than you think. In fact, money does grow on trees—the right tree, in the right place, planted the right way.

Ever Greenery

Use conifers to screen a view or just for their interesting shapes

DURING THE SUMMER, A TANGLE OF SHRUBS AND flowers creates a reasonably effective visual barrier around many properties. Come fall, however, leaves drop and the neighbor's pool looms large between the branches. That's when thoughts turn toward permanent, living screens that look as good from the back as from the front: evergreens. While evergreen refers to any plant that keeps its leaves year-round, the best view-screeners are slow-growing, cone-bearing, needle-leaved shrubs— conifers, in short.

BASIC SHAPES

Conifers may be massive or petite, growing from less than a foot high to 60 feet or more, depending on the species and variety. Shop carefully, and you can find one to fit in front of a window, for example, yet never grow up to block the view.

Conifers also come in predictable shapes. A *cone*, like the familiar Christmas tree, comes in both broad and narrow variations. A *columnar* plant, such as *Juniperus scopulorum* 'Skyrocket', will grow 20 feet tall and only 3 feet wide—like a blue-green column. The *fountain* shape suggests a weeping or cascading habit of growth; some varieties may need to be trained. *Globes* and *mounds* have a rounded appearance, and some even grow—naturally—into perfect spheres. A cone shape that spreads wide at the bottom is a *pyramid*. There are also many *spreading* evergreens on the market. These will cover an embankment or become the base for a planting of assorted conifers. Some stay as low as six inches tall without requiring a bit of shearing, clipping, or mowing.

DESIGNING WITH CONIFERS

Say good-bye to blocky hedges, clipped bowling balls, and somber green tombstones. Evergreens often have a loose informality while still retaining a tidy, controlled form throughout their lives. They look best when planted next to one another so that contrasts in their shapes, textures, and the colors of their needles—from chartreuse to steel blue—can be appreciated fully.

By tradition, a hedge is a lineup of same-species shrubs—a monoculture, like corn in the field. And therein lies its weakness. If a host species dies or insect attacks one of these plants, they all go. That's the pragmatic reason to mix species, but there's an aesthetic reason, too. A row of identical plants will not grow at identical rates in mirror-image shapes. For neatness, they will need to be trimmed once or twice a year.

Spreading: *Juniperus chinensis*

Cone: *Thuja occidentalis* 'Peabody'

SAXON HOLT (5)

Spreading: *Juniperus squamata* 'Blue Star'

Fountain: *Pinus strobus* 'Pendula'

Globe: *Platycladus orientalis* 'Aurea Nana'

On the other hand, a staggered row of small or mid-size conifers selected for their differences creates another impression. The gardener's aim is most often to be naturalistic, so variations should be enjoyed, not eliminated.

For the most natural look, plant clusters of three of each kind of conifer with an occasional individual specimen as an accent: three green cones, for example, with a golden globe at their feet. Using the basic shapes described earlier, sketch out a planting plan. Then pick the individual species that fit the plan and provide whatever variety of colors you prefer.

Fall is the best time of year to plant conifers, and it's also a good time to hunt for bargains—nurseries tend to reduce their prices in late fall, though what's left at this point may not be the cream of the crop. Decide on the shapes and ultimate heights you want. Visit local nurseries with lists in hand and ask for more suggestions. And buy the largest specimens you can afford—you'll get more satisfaction sooner from these slow growers.

A lengthy fence of conifers will not be cheap. But the gifts these handsome plants bring to the landscape are great. They can screen unsightly views, brighten a bleak winter scene, and deaden traffic noise. They can even lower winter heating bills by intercepting cold winds before they slam into your house. The challenge of working with conifers is working them into arrangements that capitalize on their utilitarian attributes.

CARE AND MAINTENANCE

Many evergreens are hardy individuals that will put up with quite a bit of neglect. With proper care, however, they will flourish. They do not usually require pruning, but make sure to remove injured or dead branches promptly, and cut back those that obstruct nearby walks or paths. Insects are rarely a problem; keeping shrubs healthy is the best defense.

Fertilize evergreens in spring with products intended specifically for them. "Be careful, though," says Roger Cook. "Improperly fertilizing some evergreens can change their color—it'll take the blue right out of a blue spruce." In drought years, supply evergreens with water—the equivalent of one inch of rainfall per week. Their roots continue to grow after the weather turns cold, which is one reason why fall is a good time to plant. The application of an antidesiccant spray to new plants helps the needles retain moisture in the winter and prevents windburn and sun scald.

Colorful Shrubs

When it comes to squeezing the most out of your landscaping dollars, it's hard to beat shrubs. Here's how to choose and plant shrubs ideal for colorful display

THE GOLDEN FLASH OF FORSYTHIA, UNRULY LIMBS splayed out at all angles, or the sweet perfume of lilacs carried on the wind. . . .These are just some of the sensory memories shrubs can elicit. Colorful shrubs command attention as they trace the progress of the seasons in a procession of blooms: yellow witch hazel blossoms, followed by blazing azaleas and lilacs, and then spirea, viburnum, and hydrangea. Color seems to fly from one bush to the next, like sparks igniting a fire.

Yet in far too many neighborhoods, you will not see such exuberant displays. They've given way to standard-issue evergreens, trendier perennials, and ornamental grasses. They all look quite nice, but the classics shouldn't be ignored. More versatile than trees, longer-lasting than perennials, and more constant than annuals, flowering shrubs pack a lot of landscaping power into a relatively small package. It takes only a few to transform a yard, whether they're used to frame a sitting area, to form a privacy hedge, or simply to stand out as a focal point in a corner of the lawn. With blooms, berries, and resplendent foliage, they can provide year-round interest in nearly every part of the country.

But if much of the gardening public has turned away from shrubs, plant breeders have remained squarely focused on them, creating a new generation of hardier, longer-lasting, and more fragrant and colorful varieties that may convince gardeners to put them in their yards. With each advance, new shrubs offer fresh landscaping possibilities and the chance to create scenes that will long be remembered.

SHOPPING FOR SHRUBS

Between the dream of a yard filled with fragrant, flowering shrubs and the day they're planted comes a trip to the nursery, where you'll find row after row of specimens ranging widely in size and cost. Tall, inexpensive plants may be the most attractive, but more important than size or cost is choosing a hearty specimen. Inspect shrubs carefully to separate the ones that are in great shape from those that may be damaged or sick.

• Check the trunk and branches for nicks or cuts, which offer inroads for disease. Reject plants with masses of thin, weak branches or blackened tips. A majority of spotted, streaked, or brown-tipped leaves could be a sign of disease, nutrient imbalance, or other stress the plant might not recover from.

• When examining a potted shrub, carefully pull off the container and look for a thick mass of light-colored, fibrous roots throughout the soil. If you see more soil than roots, or if the dirt

BURKWOOD VIBURNUM
Viburnum burkwoodii
HEIGHT: to 12 feet
ZONES: 4 to 9
Dark-green lustrous leaves turn purplish red in cold weather

SAXON HOLT

HOLLY
Ilex 'Sparkleberry'
HEIGHT: to 18 feet
ZONES: 5 to 9
Deciduous holly; produces long-lasting, bright-red fruit in winter on bare stems

ILLUSTRATIONS: MARTIN MAYO (2), MICHAEL FREEMAN (2)

SAXON HOLT

FOTHERGILLA
Fothergilla major
HEIGHT: 6–10 feet
ZONES: 5 to 8
Fragrant white
spring flowers;
bright-yellow and
orange foliage in fall

MICHAEL MacCASKEY

RUGOSA ROSES
Rosa rugosa
HEIGHT: to 10 feet
ZONES: 4 to 8
The fall payoff is
bright-red tomato-
shaped rose hips
each an inch or more
across

SAXON HOLT

easily falls away, move on to other candidates. That shrub is probably a bare-root plant recently transplanted into a container and will likely get off to a slow start; it may even require extra long-term care. With a balled-and-burlapped plant, check for tears in the fabric, an indication of possible root damage. Gently squeeze the root ball to make sure there is a firm root mass inside.

• Leaf and fruit color can vary even within one type of plant. That's why it's smart to shop for colorful plants when they're at their peak so you can choose the most vibrant ones.

• When buying shrubs for decorative fruit, remember that some plants produce berries all by themselves, while others need a pollinating plant. Each holly plant, for example, is either male or female. While the females make the berries, in most cases they need at least one male nearby for pollen. Nursery pros will instruct you on which plants need pollinators.

• Once you've settled on the types of plants you want, choose a size. In most cases, healthy smaller plants will adapt to your yard sooner and quickly catch up to larger plants. But bigger plants offer instant gratification. And whether you're buying plants in large or small containers, pass over any that are overgrown or root bound.

PLANTING A SHRUB

Most of us think of autumn as the time to begin shutting down the garden, but it's prime shrub-planting time in mild regions, where soil seldom if ever freezes. In colder regions, you can plant deciduous shrubs that are container-grown or balled-and-burlapped (bare-root plants are only available in spring) up until about a month before the ground freezes. It's safest, though, to plant them in early spring so they get the best start. At that time of year, young plants don't have to face stressful extremes, such as summer's heat and drought, and can get well established before winter—provided they are cared for.

Many gardeners think the best way to plant a shrub is in a rich mixture of peat, compost, manure, and other amendments. But that sort of pampering leads to the dreaded flowerpot effect: If the planting soil is too high powered and the surrounding soil isn't, the roots will stay put and won't venture any farther. The plant will flourish in that luxurious medium for the first year or two, but will languish after that. Better to practice a bit of tough love by digging the hole no deeper than the root ball but two to three times as wide. Instead of amending the soil, puncture the sides and bottom of the hole with a pitchfork, to allow the roots easier entry. Here are a few more pointers for planting shrubs from containers, which is how most are sold:

• Before putting in the shrubs, dig a hole and fill it halfway with water. If there is still water in it after two hours, find a spot with better drainage. This may sound like a lot of extra work, but filling in a hole or two is a lot easier (and less expensive) than replacing a shrub down the road.

• Don't plant too deeply. By planting at the proper depth, you will prevent water from collecting on the roots of a shrub or at the base of the plant, which can cause decay or root suffocation. Your nursery can tell you the depth suited for each plant.

• Remove a potted shrub from its container or peel away the fabric from a balled-and-burlapped plant. If the roots are crowded and growing around each other, gently tease them apart.

• To prevent the plant from settling, place plants in their hole on a plateau of compacted or undisturbed soil.

• Place the plant in the hole, and carefully refill it with native soil. Lightly tamp the dirt, soak it with water, and add a 2-inch-deep layer of mulch, keeping it away from the trunk. Pour on a weak solution of liquid fertilizer, and water well once a week for the first month. "But follow label instructions carefully," says Roger Cook, "or you'll end up doing more harm than good."

• After planting and watering, spread a 2- to 4-inch layer of organic mulch around the shrubs. But be sure to keep the mulch away from the plant base. Mulch applied up against trunks or stems can rot the bark and girdle the plant. It also creates entry points for insects and disease organisms.

MATCHING SHRUBS TO YOUR YARD

When someone mentions garden color, you probably think of scarlet oaks, sugar maples, and other tall, majestic shade trees in their vibrant autumn best. Unfortunately, most of us just don't have room for these giants. A sugar maple, for example, grows to 80 feet high with equal spread—big enough to overwhelm many yards.

Shrubs, on the other hand, are a natural for today's smaller properties. Many offer a spectacular fall display of leaves, fruit, and berries, along with a bonus of flowers in spring. Most also cost less than trees, mature more quickly and are colorful the first fall season after planting. And because shrubs are permanent, they're especially useful as screens, barriers, and ground covers. Best of all, chosing and planting shrubs that blaze with

PEEGEE HYDRANGEA
Hydrangea paniculata
HEIGHT: 10–20 feet
ZONES: 4 to 8
Large, creamy-white flower clusters in late summer that fade to bronze in autumn, and persist into winter

MICHAEL MacCASKEY

PERSIAN LILAC
Syringa x persica
HEIGHT: 6 feet
ZONES: 5 to 8
Profusion of compact, fragrant purple flowers that bloom in late spring

ILLUSTRATIONS: MARTIN MAYO (4)

SAXON HOLT

VIBURNUM
*Viburnum
dilatatum* 'Erie'
HEIGHT: 6–9 feet
ZONES: 5 to 8
Red fruits that appear at
end of summer and turn
coral-pink with first frost

MICHAEL MacCASKEY

**CHINESE
SNOWBALL**
*Viburnum
macrocephalum*
HEIGHT: 12–15 feet
ZONES: 7 to 9
Huge balls of flowers in
late spring that turn
from chartreuse to white

SAXON HOLT

color and look great year-round doesn't require a degree in horticulture.

Don't choose shrubs based solely on fall color or any other single feature. You're likely to get a beautiful plant that won't grow well or look good in your yard. Instead, determine the growing conditions you're working with. Then choose shrubs that thrive in them without constant coddling. Here are some questions to answer before you start digging:

• How cold does your weather get? The ability of a plant to tolerate a minimum temperature is called hardiness. Although hardiness can vary somewhat with growing conditions, knowing how cold it gets where you live allows you to choose plants adapted to your climate. If you don't know the minimum winter temperature in your area, check with the staff of an area nursery or the local extension service.

• What's the pH of your soil? Have the soil tested by the extension service; tests are inexpensive. Does the soil stay waterlogged or does it dry out quickly? Does it feel sandy, or firm and sticky like clay? Some shrubs, including red chokeberry and cotoneaster, tolerate a wide range of soils. Others have specific needs, such as acidic soil or excellent drainage. Often, nursery displays and labels describe the specific soil requirements for a plant.

• Sun or shade? What direction does the site face? How much sunlight does it receive during the day and through the seasons? Some shrubs, such as fothergilla and oakleaf hydrangea, grow well either in sun or partial shade. With most shrubs, however, fall color is more intense and fruit and berries more abundant in sun.

• Is the ground level or steep, and how exposed is it to prevailing winds? Fragrant sumac is among the shrubs with great fall color that tolerate a broad range of conditions, including wind. It also helps stabilize slopes because its stems root where they touch the ground.

• How large is the planting area? Don't plant a shrub that grows 12 feet in all directions in a 4×4-foot space. Most shrubs look best and fruit more heavily when allowed to reach their natural size and shape. And, you'll avoid spending some of your weekends pruning.

To get the most from fall-color shrubs, look at each plant's function within the landscape. For example, midsize shrubs create a smooth transition between trees and flower beds or lawn. Tall, dense shrubs massed together screen views and provide plenty of privacy.

Pay attention to foliage texture and size as well as color. Both determine the overall appearance of a shrub and how well it complements neighboring plants. Highlight individual shrubs by mixing types with contrasting textures.

Plant shrubs with multiseasonal appeal. Witch hazel, for example, dons spiderlike, yellow-red flowers in fall, winter, or early spring and displays fall foliage in a kaleidoscope of warm colors. You can also mix shrubs with varied peak seasons for color year-round.

Finally, avoid the jarring polka-dot look created by planting one each of several different kinds of shrubs. Make your landscape more harmonious by grouping several shrubs of the same type within a planting or repeating them throughout the landscape.

SHRUBS FOR COLOR

You'll find a variety of colorful shrubs in the photos on these pages. But there are other shrubs to consider, too. They're easy to maintain and widely available where they're hardy. And you'll surely come up with additional choices if you check with neighbors and local experts. Plants in the following list are deciduous, unless noted; temperatures are in degrees Fahrenheit.

Cranberry bush (*Viburnum trilobum*) gets its common name from its showy red, autumn fruit. White spring flowers in flat lacy clusters precede the fruit. Maplelike leaves turn yellow to red purple in fall. This shrub grows to 15 feet high and wide. The variety 'Compactum' grows 6 feet tall. European cranberry bush, *V. opulus*, is a related shrub that's similar in appearance. Hardy to -50°.

Cranberry cotoneaster (*Cotoneaster apiculatus*) is a low, spreading shrub 3 feet high and 3 to 6 feet wide. Its dark, glossy-green summer foliage turns shades of red or purple in autumn. White or pinkish springtime flowers are followed by bright-red berries that ripen in late summer and usually last for several months. Hardy to -30°.

Dwarf fothergilla (*Fothergilla gardenii*) is grown principally for its intense yellow and orange-red fall foliage. Honey-scented white flowers in brushlike, 1- to 2-inch clusters in spring are another outstanding feature. Plants typically reach 2 to 3 feet high with a 3-foot spread. *F. major* is a related species similar to *F. gardenii* but larger, growing to 9 feet. These shrubs prefer acid soil. Hardy to -30°.

Firethorns (*Pyracantha*) are a group of shrubs unrivaled for their breathtaking fall fruit. Depending on species and variety, the large, dense clusters of pea-size fruit are orange, red, or yellow. Sizes and shapes vary from sprawling ground covers up to 18-foot high plants. Nearly all varieties feature

JAPANESE BARBERRY
Berberis thunbergii
HEIGHT: to 6 feet
ZONES: 4 to 9
Small rounded leaves turn yellow, orange, and red in fall

BEAUTY BUSH
Kolkwitzia amabilis
HEIGHT: 6–15 feet
ZONES: 5 to 9
Fountains of pink flowers with yellow thoats appear in late spring; bark exfoliates as shrub matures

ILLUSTRATIONS: MARTIN MAYO (2), MICHAEL FREEMAN (2)

SAXON HOLT (4)

OAK LEAF HYDRANGEA

Hydrangea quercifolia

HEIGHT: 4–6 feet
ZONES: 4 to 9
Fragrant yellow flowers can last from summer to early fall

BUTTERCUP WINTER HAZEL

Corylopsis pauciflora

HEIGHT: 4–6 feet
ZONES: 6 to 9
Soft yellow flowers in early spring; handsome foliage all spring and summer

needlelike thorns. Leaves are evergreen to semi-deciduous in cold climates. Hardiness varies.

Fragrant sumac (*Rhus araomatica*) grows 3 to 5 feet tall and sprawls much wider than that. Its attractive, glossy-green 3-inch leaves are fragrant when brushed against or crushed. Fall leaf color in oranges, reds and purples lasts for several weeks. The 'Grow-low' variety reaches only 2 feet high and spreads 6 to 8 feet. Hardy to -40°.

Heavenly bamboo (*Nandina domestica*) is a feathery, upright 6- to 8-foot shrub, though it can easily be kept smaller. White flowers appear in midsummer, followed by orange-red pea-size fruit in fall. Fine-textured foliage is glossy green in summer, becoming reddish purple in fall and sometimes brilliant red in winter. This shrub is evergreen in all but the coldest part of its range. Low-growing varieties are available. Hardy to 0°.

Purple beautyberry (*Callicarpa dichotoma*) is known for its spectacular fall clusters of ⅛-inch lilac-violet fruit. These graceful plants with arching branches reach 4 feet tall and wider. They will freeze to the ground in cold-winter areas, but come back from the roots. *Callicarpa d. albifructus* is a white-fruited form. Hardy to -20°.

Red chokeberry (*Aronia*) grows 6 to 8 feet high and spreads 3 to 5 feet. Abundant bright-red fruit develop along branches in late summer and stay well into winter. Fall leaf color is a bright red purple and lasts for several weeks. Black chokeberry (*A. melanocarpa*) is similar, but ripe fruit is blackish purple. Hardy to -30°.

Summersweet (*Clethra alnifolia*) grows 10 feet tall with vertical branches that are thin but strong. In summer, tiny fragrant white flowers bloom on branch tips in spires 4 to 6 inches long. The 2- to 4-inch-long leaves turn yellow to gold in fall. Hardy to -40°.

Winged euonymus (*Euonymus alata*) is prized for its fiery-red fall foliage. Also called burning bush, it grows 15 to 20 feet high and wide. The variety 'Compacta' reaches 6 to 10 feet high. Hardy to -30°.

Winterberry (*Ilex verticillata*) bears a generous bounty of bright-red fruit that ripens in fall and can last all winter. Plants grow 6 to 10 feet tall with oval leaves 3-inches long. 'Red Sprite' is a dwarf variety reaching 4 feet. Hardy to -30°.

Witch hazel (*Hamamelis intermedia*) grows to 15 feet high with an equal or greater spread. Fall color can be yellow, orange, and red on the same plant. Or it can be a single color depending on variety. Spiderlike winter flowers on bare stems range from yellow to oranges to reds. Hardy to -20°.

Privet Hedge

A nearly indestructible wall of privacy that grows more than a foot a year

SURROUNDED BY A FEATURELESS EXPANSE OF SEA, ISLAND inhabitants seem to crave a cozy definition of their outdoor space. On Nantucket, a small island off the coast of Massachusetts, this purpose is accomplished by the liberal use of privet. Crisply trimmed privet hedges mark off lawns and gardens, and privet arches serve as living gateways. The best are grown in the island's village of Sconset, and often as topiary. Where else would privet whales with privet spouts be more suitable?

"Privet is a living fence," says Nantucket landscaper Marty McGowan, "and the more you prune it, the thicker it gets." Although the Oxford English Dictionary lists "origin unknown" for the common name of the genus *Ligustrum*, McGowan ventures an etymological leap: "It must have something to do with privacy," he says. "That's what privet is all about."

Privet has evergreen and deciduous varieties, all relatives of the olive. The privet commonly used for hedges and topiary in temperate regions is *Ligustrum ovalifolium*, or California privet, which is hardy to about zero degrees Fahrenheit. California privet and the even more cold-hardy *L. amurense* (or Amur privet, from east Asia) are deciduous. Their shiny, dark-green leaves can remain on branches well into early winter; in summer, sprays of small white blossoms appear unless the plants have been pruned severely.

Spouting whales aside, when most people think of privet, they think of hedges. Privet "grows up more than out," says McGowan, and this natural tendency, combined with the plant's dense foliage, will generate an opaque screen within a few years.

McGowan recommends planting privet in a trench 2 feet wide and 18 to 24 inches deep. Space plants 1 foot apart, and cover the roots in soil right up to the point where the trunk begins to branch. "Privet is one of those plants, like tomatoes, that will put a root out of its side anywhere it's in contact with soil," McGowan says.

Because it's so fast-growing in either sun or shade, privet can become a pest. Kris Johnson, supervisory naturalist for the Great Smoky Mountains National Park in Tennessee and North Carolina, says her crews have spent many hours eradicating the plant. "It can really take over the forest," she says. "Don't plant it next to a meadow or woodlot." Mowing alongside a hedge will keep it in bounds, and regular clipping will prevent formation of seeds that birds might spread.

PRUNING

Pruning a privet hedge is neither an arcane science nor a full-time career. All branches should have access to sunlight. McGowan favors pruning in an upside-down V shape—wider at the bottom

This privet hedge adds privacy and helps the transition from the sidewalk to the house.

Topiary is used to separate and define beds of red and yellow marigolds.

than at the top. "If you do it the other way around, the branches at the bottom will die from not getting enough sun." Most hedge fanciers favor level tops, which allow sunlight to fall evenly on the top branches, where 70 percent of new growth occurs. Two cuttings per growing season are usually enough; a finer, chiseled look might require three or four.

Nantucket doesn't allow man-made fences to be more than six feet high, but there's no restriction on the height of a hedge. One 20-footer on Main Street in Sconset got that big in 18 years. Nearby, a privet allée is commodious enough to let cars pass beneath. As for Moby Dick out in the backyard, he can grow as large as he likes. ■

LEFT: **A box-wood hedge and topiary flank the gravel walk of this formal garden.**

SAXON HOLT (3)

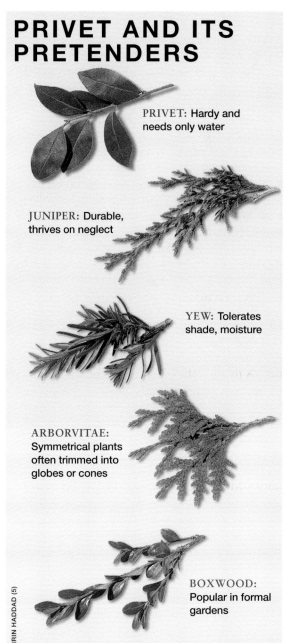

PRIVET AND ITS PRETENDERS

PRIVET: Hardy and needs only water

JUNIPER: Durable, thrives on neglect

YEW: Tolerates shade, moisture

ARBORVITAE: Symmetrical plants often trimmed into globes or cones

BOXWOOD: Popular in formal gardens

DARRIN HADDAD (5)

Choosing Vines

Climbers, clingers, and ramblers will cover a trellis, an arbor, or even a shed roof with profuse color

V INES ARE PLANTS ON THE GO. VERTICALLY INCLINED and born to run, they bridge the gap between earth and sky as they soften hard landscape features. Whether energetic annuals or slower-growing perennials, vines can enliven a trellis or pergola with their lush greenery or shelter an outdoor eating area. Growing up a fence or wall, vines provide a verdant backdrop for flower borders in the garden. They can give a lift to a plain-Jane house or disguise an architectural flaw, and lightweight vines can be used to hide unsightly necessities, such as electric meters and gutter downspouts.

Deciduous vines even offer climate control: In summer, their leaves will cover walls or a lattice set against a house and keep heat off walls. After the leaves drop, welcome warmth penetrates the spaces between their stems. A vine trained to entwine a pergola, like the wisteria shown at right, can filter bright light, provide privacy, and muffle neighborhood noise.

HOW VINES CLIMB

Vines look best when properly trained to a support that will accommodate their growing habits. Because annuals live out their brief lives in only a season, they are fast growing and prolific. They are typically lighter in weight than perennial vines, which develop thick, woody stems over the years.

Twiners (see page 82), such as the annual morning glory and hyacinth bean, readily wrap their stems around a string or wire, or a more sturdy structure. They also make a terrific camouflage for chain-link fencing, but will ramble over a nearby shrub if not kept in check. Perennial twiners such as kiwi and wisteria should be anchored on a strong structure—a pergola with concrete footings or a sturdy porch, for instance—that won't collapse under the weight of the mature plant's heavy, ropy stems.

Clingers (see page 82), such as climbing hydrangea, use sticky holdfasts or hairy rootlets to grab onto their supports; they prosper on any sturdy structure.

Grabbers (see page 83), like sweet pea, use their delicate tendrils or, like passionflower, their leaf stalks to attach themselves to virtually any surface.

Leaners, like roses, must be fastened to some sort of a support as they grow.

A profusion of wisteria blossoms add shade and privacy to this pathway.

SAXON HOLT (2)

It's a good idea to avoid growing a vine directly on your house, however. Vines that climb by means of sticky holdfasts similar to suction cups will damage brick, mortar, stucco, and wood. Instead, train them on a structure that can be pulled away from the house when you must paint or make repairs. This could be a trellis or even an old wooden ladder. Another alternative is to attach a grid of wires to the wall with galvanized eyehooks, allowing 1 or 2 inches of breathing room between the vine and the house exterior.

VINES TO AVOID

Vines are vigorous growers, some notoriously so. Kudzu—brought from Japan in the 19th century to the southern United States—will smother whatever stands in its path. Even some nursery plants will take over unless you keep them in check. These include five-leaf akebia, oriental bittersweet, porcelain berry, trumpet vine, and Japanese honeysuckle.

If one of these vines is growing in your yard, there are three surefire ways to limit its mischief: (1) Kill it with an herbicide, unearth it, and replace it with a vine that has a reputation for good citizenship. (2) Prune it severely and repeatedly. Cut its main stems nearly to the ground each fall or late winter, then remove excess sprouts and suckers periodically over the growing season to limit its spread. (3) Snip off all flowers before they develop seeds.

DESIGNING WITH VINES

Nancy Goodwin has spent more than two decades shaping the landscape at Montrose, her property on the outskirts of Hillsborough, North Carolina. Widely respected among horticulturists, Goodwin jokes that she and her husband, Craufurd, purchased Montrose and its lovely Georgian-style house "for the dirt," but she fervently believes that even the smallest garden plot should have at least one element that reaches for the sky.

If a garden is absolutely flat, as part of hers was originally, there is nothing to prompt exploration, no place to rest, nothing to lure the visitor from one area to another. Even in a small garden, an arbor rising over a bench offers visitors the same experience.

Trellis walls can partition a landscape into a series of garden rooms, much as walls do within a house, or they can be used to screen unsightly

TOP: This arbor, covered in honeysuckle, frames and focuses a view into the yard beyond.
RIGHT: Bougainvillea on a wood trellis.

SAXON HOLT (2)

ABOVE: Wrought-iron supports give loofah-gourd vine, gloriosa lily, and climbing snapdragons a foothold on the column of a porch.
LEFT: Vines are ideal for softening hard edges.

views, such as those of a neighbor's trash cans. An opening in a trellis, or a graceful arch, might frame a vista of a swimming pool or a pond, or set off a garden accessory—a birdbath, perhaps, or an urn brimming with flowers. But resist the temptation to let vines overwhelm the structure. "Otherwise," says Goodwin, "the beauty of the frame disappears and so does the view beyond it."

Not all vertical elements have to tower above the ground. A waist-high fence festooned with rambling roses works the same way a sofa placed at an angle to a wall might direct traffic through the room. Both serve to reroute visitors, though only one will encourage them to slow down a bit and enjoy the journey.

Goodwin says there's an easy, homemade way to figure out how high and wide a simple vine support should be. All you need are two friends, two lightweight poles, such as those used to stake beans, and string to tie between the poles. Position the two "pole bearers" where the edges of the structure might go, then have them move the poles around to test desirable widths and heights.

Vines will grow up most any material, from pliable willow to durable wrought iron. The choice will be affected by the type of climbing plants or vines you plan to train to cover the structure. Weighty climbers like wisteria, which has been

SEEKING THE SUN

CLINGERS Features include suction-cup disks, aerial roots, or hooklike claws along the stems that attach to flat surfaces. Examples include Boston ivy (ABOVE), and English ivy.

TWINERS The entire stem twists and spirals around a support as it grows. Examples include clematis (ABOVE), bittersweet, honeysuckle, and wisteria.

known to pull down a 50-foot tree, require more support than a delicate vine such as sweet pea.

If you want your vertical garden to be constructed of wood, consider redwood and cedar—they work well most anywhere. Goodwin sometimes uses preservative-treated pine and doesn't bother with paint or stain. "Wood ages in the most beautiful way," she says. "But the most important thing is the flowers embroidering the form."

Although a trellis or arbor may look painfully bare when first installed, a few well-chosen vining annuals can soften its contours for the short term. Most perennial vines take three years to establish themselves, so annuals should continue to be planted alongside until the perennial vines take hold.

Many perennial vines must be trained to climb. Stout string or chicken wire works well, or you can enclose some plants in tepees to help guide the young vine for a season or two. As climbers grow, weave them around the framework of your garden structure to encourage them to cover it evenly. Routine watering, pruning, and training of errant vines should ensure that the perennial cover will last for years.

CHOOSING VINES

Perennial climbers will give you pleasure year after year. Here are a few suggestions for plants that can be grown almost anywhere within Zones 3–8, which encompasses most of the United States. Zones 9 and 10, the southernmost zones, range from humid, tropical conditions to hot, dry desert; tropical climbers do best in pots in cooler zones. Consult your local nursery regarding the particular zone and the availability and suitability of plants for your vertical garden.

• Dutchman's Pipe: Large, heart-shaped leaves for decorative screening; small yellowish-green flowers.

• Trumpet Vine: Vigorous grower; orange-red flowers attract hummingbirds.

GRABBERS Growths along stems or at leaf ends reach out and twine around objects to support the rest of the plant. Examples include grape (ABOVE), passionflower, and trumpet vine.

• Wisteria: Ornamental vine with showy, fragrant pea-like flowers.

• Honeysuckle: Fragrant vine that can grow nationwide. However, some types are invasive and should be avoided.

• Golden Trumpet Vine: Large yellow flowers; prolific bloomer.

• Madagascar Jasmine: Sparsely branched with small white flowers; intensely fragrant; long bloom period.

CLIMBING ROSES

Roses used as vines are called climbing roses. Technically, though, they may be climbers or ramblers. Both categories contain dozens of varieties that will trail along fences, clamber up trellises, or encircle lampposts. Climbing roses generally grow to a height of 8 to 10 feet, which is ideal for most structures, and flower at least twice from early summer into fall; some new varieties bloom continuously throughout the growing season. Ramblers can grow to a vigorous 15 to 25 feet tall and typically bloom just once a year.

Despite their shorter bloom duration and sometimes unwieldy growing habit, ramblers are worth planting where you've got the space, says Larry Parton, a longtime rose grower and owner of the Northland Rosarium in Spokane, Washington. Not only will they grow taller and cover more area than climbers, but they also flower much more profusely, unfolding a spectacular show for three to six weeks in spring (the cooler the weather, the longer they'll stay in bloom). Like rhododendrons and azaleas, roses that bloom just once mark the seasons, arriving in splendor, giving joy to the heart, and then going away—only to be awaited and welcomed once more a year hence. "They also tend to be hardier and more disease-resistant than those that bloom all season," adds Parton.

No roses cling to a surface on their own, however, and some need more support than others. Climbing roses must be tied up to keep them from blowing or falling over. And while ramblers tend to grow thickly and heavily enough to stay put once they're established, tying them in place for the first couple of years is the best way to train them over a structure.

In either case, you should immobilize three or four primary canes, says Parton. To do so, he uses plastic garden tape, which can be found at any nursery. The tape is strong and flexible, so it's unlikely to damage canes even in a hard wind. Twine also works but is less forgiving, and the natural fibers can decompose in a year or two. "Don't use wire," Parton warns—it can bite into rose canes and kill them. Tie the tape or twine tightly to the support, then loosely to the canes. If necessary, you can place hooks into wood or even masonry substrates and tie the canes to those. (When it comes time to repaint a wall or fence, simply lift off the cane and lay it on the ground.)

Unless routinely pruned, ramblers can quickly develop into a tangled mass. Climbers are more restrained, but still benefit from annual trimming to keep a pleasing shape and encourage blooming. "Don't be timid. Roses are tough and grow back fast," Parton says. "Save the main canes, then do what looks good." Always cut above a bud that points to the outside of the bush; this prevents new canes from growing into the middle.

All roses have one overriding characteristic: "They need sunlight to bloom," Parton says. That means at least six to eight hours of sun on a clear day. The payoff for proper placement, though, is tremendous. These exuberant bloomers add a heart-stopping grace note to the landscape. ■

Building a Wood Pergola

Helping vines reach for the sky

CLIMBING ROSES AND VINES LOOK GREAT GROWING on anything, but a pergola—a horizontal wood trellis supported by columns—provides the ideal framework on which to showcase their rambunctious beauty. A pergola doesn't take up much space but it yields big results, making it a perfect choice for the small yard at a *This Old House* project in West Palm Beach, Florida. The pergola runs from a house to the adjacent guest house, providing a gateway that frames a Tuscany-inspired poolscape—a fitting choice, because pergolas were popular in ancient Rome.

Master carpenter Norm Abram built the 9-foot-tall assembly on site using basic carpentry tools and a bandsaw. The assembly consists of a 16-foot-long beam crossed by 10 riblike crosspieces, each 5 feet long. They, in turn, are topped with seven perpindicular rails running the length of the beam. Norm used cedar for the project—it's an easily worked and readily available wood particularly suited to use outdoors.

Inspired by a detail at the end of the house rafters, Norm cut an ogee design on both ends of the beam and on the ends of all the crosspieces. To maintain a consistent shape, he traced it using a template (step 1). Feeding such thick stock into a bandsaw, however, would have been tough, so instead he immobilized the lumber and maneuvered the saw—set on casters—like a giant saber saw.

Each crosspiece was attached to the beam every 16 inches using a half-lap joint, created by notching the beam and crosspiece so they mate together like Lincoln Logs. To create the notches, Norm used a circular saw to cut a series of 1½-inch-deep kerfs in the wood, then knocked away the waste (step 2) and smoothed surfaces with a hand plane and chisel. The notches made assembly easy (step 3). All Norm had to do was make sure that each crosspiece sat squarely on the beam.

A single, countersunk lag screw, 8 inches long, fastened each crosspiece to the beam (step 4). The holes were filled later with a cedar plug. Finally, Norm secured the 2×2 rails with marine-grade adhesive and a handful of 3-inch hot-dipped galvanized screws (step 5).

It took the combined efforts of Norm and seven helpers to lift the assembled pergola atop two steel posts (step 6), where it was secured with 6-inch-long lag screws. Eventually, the posts would be transformed into classically-styled faux-stone columns when they were wrapped by cast-concrete sheaths. ■

STEP 1: Norm uses a template to trace an ogee shape on the ends of the 3×8 crosspieces.

STEP 2: After making repeated crosscuts with a circular saw, Norm knocked out the waste, then smoothed the notch.

STEP 4: A single lag bolt holds each crosspiece in place. Each counterbored hole is covered by a top rail.

STEP 3: Before fastening each crosspiece, Norm squared it to the beam.

STEP 5: The top rails were spaced evenly and fastened to the crosspieces.

STEP 6: When the pergola "rack" was complete, Norm (with lots of help) lifted it onto two steel structural posts anchored in concrete.

Choosing Ground Covers

Don't let shady conditions ruin your yard. These attractive low-maintenance plants thrive in low light

IF, AS THE SAYING GOES, IT'S IMPORTANT TO PICK YOUR BATTLES, then trying to grow grass in shade just isn't worth the fight. Turf needs lots of light to thrive. Without three to four hours of direct sunlight each day or a full day of filtered light, a lawn becomes thin or spotty and, inevitably, weeds and disease make keeping the grass alive a headache.

Rather than fight the loosing battle, replace the lawn with ground covers that do well in low light. You will not only cover spots where nothing grew before, but you will also add color and texture to your yard. Just remember that though ground covers can do a lot that grass can't, none provide the tough play surface of turf. Very few can handle even light foot traffic. If you plan to walk through a ground cover area with any regularity, create a footpath using stepping-stones.

CHOOSING THE RIGHT PLANT

As with any type of plant, match the ground cover to the growing conditions in your yard. The plants featured here do well in shady areas, but not all will grow in deep shade (where little or no sun reaches the ground during the day). For these dark areas, consider pachysandra, one of the most reliable evergreen ground covers. The less common wild gingers, with their heart-shaped leaves, are another good choice, as are foam flowers, which bloom in spring.

Some ground covers spread by underground runners or root along the soil as they grow. These types, such as English ivy, tend to be aggressive growers and should be separated from other plants or used in an area where they are free to spread without consequences. Others, like wild ginger and hostas, spread slowly by clumps and are more controllable.

Many yards include one or more of the following problem areas. Be sure to choose the right plant for the each situation.

Slopes Fast-growing ground covers that root as they spread are valuable plants for shady slopes, especially those too steep or rocky to mow. English ivy, for one, actually knits soil together with its roots and helps prevent erosion. Many varieties of this plant are available, giving you a choice of leaf size, texture, and color.

Ajuga and common periwinkle (*Vinca minor*) also cover slopes well. If you live in a cold climate, the plants' hardiness may determine your final choice: Ajuga is hardy to -40°F, common periwinkle to -30°F, and English ivy to -20°F.

RIGHT: This blooming shade garden with mixed ground covers thrives under a dogwood.
BELOW: Redwood sorrel (*Oxalis oregana*) works well in shade.

SAXON HOLT (2)

SAXON HOLT

Dry shade Dry shade is one of the most challenging gardening situations. It's common under large trees with shallow roots that take water from the soil surface. While most plants prefer moist soil, some will tolerate dry shade. For example, barrenwort (*Epimedium*) is a slow-spreading

Hostas are ideal underneath deciduous trees, where their bold leaves in varied colors, sizes, and shapes contrast with one another and the bark of the trees.

ground cover with beautiful light-green, heart-shaped leaves that turn a reddish color in fall. Small flowers in loose sprays bloom in spring on plants 8 to 12 inches high. These plants are especially attractive as a small-scale ground cover in a woodland setting.

Spring-flowering foam flower works well in north-facing spots.

Lilyturfs also take dry shade. They form clumps of grasslike leaves up to 18 inches long and produce white or lavender summer flowers. Also consider some of the hostas. One variety useful in dry shade is 'Ginko Craig'. It has elongated frosty-green leaves edged in white.

Soggy soil At the other end of the spectrum are damp low-lying areas where drainage is poor and soil stays moist. Well adapted for this situation is dwarf Chinese astilbe (*Astilbe chinensis* 'Pumila'), a mat-forming plant with fernlike leaves and 12-inch spikes of mauve flowers that bloom in late summer.

For colorful foliage, try variegated houttuynia, an aggressive spreader with heart-shaped leaves in combinations of green, red, yellow, and cream. Established plantings are tough to eradicate, so use it only where spreading won't be a problem.

Another good ground-hugging spreader is creeping Jenny. It has shiny round leaves and bright-yellow flowers. Keep it away from lawn and other plants, however, because it too can be invasive. The yellow-leafed variety 'Aurea' is less aggressive.

PLANTING STRATEGIES

With a good start, ground covers will develop dense, weed-choking foliage as they grow. But if weeds got there first, you'll have to get rid of them. If you use chemicals, consider nonselective herbicides, such as Roundup (glyphosate) and Finale (glufosinate-ammonium). Apply either one to green weeds a few weeks before you plant the ground cover. After planting, spread organic mulch 2 to 4 inches deep between plants to keep weeds from reestablishing themselves.

Most shade-dwelling plants prefer rich soil high in organic matter. When planting in open ground with small plants from packs or flats, work a 2- to 3-inch layer of compost or composted manure into the top 6 to 8 inches of soil over the entire area. When planting under trees, instead of disturbing or covering surface roots, place organic matter in pockets of soil between the roots, then plant in those pockets.

If you're planting ground covers from larger 1- or 2-gallon containers, add amendments to the individual planting holes rather than working the entire planting site. This method works better on steep slopes as well, because it minimizes erosion problems.

This planting of mixed ground covers includes barrenwort (*Epimedium*), foam flower (*Tiarella*), and ferns.

English ivy (*Hedera helix*) flanks this brick walkway on both sides.

Plant small plants from packs or flats by digging a hole that's just deep enough for the root ball. Place the plant so the top of the root ball is even with the soil surface. To plant a ground cover that comes in a large container, taper each hole outward at the base and create a plateau for the root ball to sit on. The top of the root ball should end up just slightly above soil level.

If you're planting on a slope, set the plant on its own terrace or level spot and make a shallow watering basin around the outer edge of the root ball. Again, the root ball should be slightly above grade. Erosion controls include planting in a triangular or staggered pattern, and creating a terrace for each plant. Or you can install biodegradable jute netting over the soil. A layer of mulch spread after planting also helps break the force of rainfall or irrigation water. If a slope is steep and the underlying soil is unstable, call a soils engineer or landscape architect before planting—

SAXON HOLT (4)

The small round leaves of creeping Jenny (*Lysimachia nummularia*) form a lush, low carpet.

Pachysandra, ferns, and trillium are combined to create this natural looking garden.

nobody wants to see fresh plantings slide down the hillside after the first soaking rain.

Water new plants well and spread a couple of inches of organic mulch on the bare ground between them. Mulch helps control weeds and, as it decomposes, it also improves the soil. Continue to water regularly until the plants start to fill in.

ONGOING CARE

As ground covers become established, less upkeep is required. Watering and weeding remain "as needed" chores. Watering requirements will depend on a number of factors, including plant type, climate. and soil considerations. Most plantings need weeding for the first two years.

Many nonwoody ground covers, including ajuga and common periwinkle, benefit from annual mowing or shearing. This rejuvenates the plants and keeps them looking fresh. Others, such as English ivy and pachysandra, are renewed by mowing every few years in spring.

Various ground covers can become crowded in time or, in some cases, sections will begin to die out. When this occurs, dig up the weak plants and fill in bare spots with divisions of healthy plants.

If this sounds like a lot of work, keep in mind that well-chosen, established ground covers require much less maintenance than lawn. A good start is what they need most to look great for years to come. ◼

PLACING AND SPACING

The ideal planting distance between ground covers varies between a couple of inches to a couple of feet. The spacing depends on the specific plant and, to some extent, how quickly you want it to fill in. The closer the spacing, the sooner plants will cover the area and suppress weeds. Check plant tags for recommended spacing.

Keep these tips in mind when placing plants:

• Arrange plants in staggered rows rather than in line with one another. This setup gives a more natural impression and helps control erosion.

• Ground covers work and look best when planted in large groups, not when lined up in a single row.

• Massing a single species (RIGHT) gives a more formal appearance and is easier to maintain.

• Add interest to large areas by planting two or more kinds of ground cover in drifts side by side, blending them at the edges. This requires extra planning and upkeep, but it let's you mix and match plants of varying colors and heights, and choose varieties that flower at different times. Don't use an aggressive plant next to a timid one, or one may crowd out the other.

Ground cover of pachysandra creates a bed of lush greenery and directs the eye to a gazebo.

The Yard Planned

The best foundation planting plan embraces the whole yard

ALTHOUGH IT WAS DECOROUS AMERICANS OF THE Victorian era who first felt compelled to cover a house's naked foundation with shrubbery, it was the post-World War II builders of tract houses who gave such plantings a bad name. Nineteenth-century homeowners carefully selected from a wide range of shrubs, ivies, and other evergreens to dress up their facades, but to add instant curb appeal to barren suburban landscapes and cover slab or concrete-block foundations inexpensively, "builders leaned on just a few types of fast-growing shrubs," says Tom Wirth, a Sherborn, Massachusetts–based landscape architect who has designed many residential landscapes for *This Old House*. As time passed and the shrubs sprawled, "people became used to the idea of having their homes surrounded by plants," he says. Contemporary landscape professionals have a nickname for the uninspired and overgrown look of American front yards: "cover and smother." New thinking aims for a cleaner approach. "Many houses do not require dense coverage," says Wirth. "Instead, landscape architects design plantings that take the entire yard into account, including the driveway, boundaries shared with neighbors, and paths between the sidewalk and the house."

In suburban Massachusetts, Wirth has many opportunities to practice what he preaches. Early one summer, he was asked to landscape a single-story ranch home in Needham that a couple had recently purchased for the wife's elderly parents, the Nixons. The house (photo, far right) was almost completely shrouded by gangly rhododendrons and overgrown yews, and blocked by a leggy hawthorn and several heavy, low-hanging branches of a beautiful but enormous sugar maple.

A top priority, in Wirth's opinion, was to make the house look more inviting and attractive from the sidewalk and street. Another, in response to his clients' desire, was to give the homeowners plantings that would be texturally interesting to look out on. Because the Nixons spent most of their time indoors, thay wanted a lovely yard that they could enjoy from windows in the family room and dining nook. "Curb appeal is only part of the picture," says Wirth. "How you view the property from inside is just as important."

The design that evolves from this premise will factor in many conditions and needs. "There are several subtle points to con-

The finished front-yard planting received a 2- to 4-inch layer of bark mulch, to hold moisture. Until plants are established, they will have to be watered weekly. The plantings seem sparse now, but will eventually fill in. Says *This Old House* landscape contractor Roger Cook: "We purposely put in plants that would look better as time goes by."

sider besides the way the landscape looks at the moment," says Sara Jane von Trapp, a Redding, Connecticut, landscape designer who managed her own nursery and landscaping business in Vermont for 17 years. "Climate conditions, the orientation of the house, and the lay of the land are just three. You should also make note of the architectural features of your house, as well as how you access it. If you have two doors, you may want to emphasize one and downplay the other with the planting design. Also, do you need extra shade or noise protection? And, do you have to take kids or pets—or pesky critters that are invading yards nearby—into account?"

Some considerations may not be readily apparent until an on-site assessment occurs. Signe Nielsen, a landscape architect from New York City with over 25 years of experience, mentions other practical concerns. "Air-conditioning condensing units, electric and gas meters, and satellite dishes are just as ugly as an exposed foundation," she says. She also inquires about repairs made to the house that might affect the quality of the soil. If the siding has been acid washed, for example, some of the liquid might have leached into the soil, making it too acidic; if bricks have been repointed, the soil will be too alkaline. In cases such as these, she tests the soil.

ASSESSING THE SITUATION

When Wirth went to work at the Nixon's property to assess the existing conditions, he was accompanied by Roger Cook, who'd be performing the work at the site. The men examined each individual specimen plant to ascertain

It was clear that the overgrown front yard of the house needed work.

whether it should be pruned and retained in its present position, transplanted to another location in the yard, or removed entirely. "Most people are protective of their existing plants," Nielsen says. "I always tell my clients not to be afraid to start anew." At the Nixons', Wirth and Cook agreed that most of the plants were overgrown and poorly shaped, and had to go. "But if there's anything worthwhile, we believe in saving it," Roger says. That doesn't necessarily mean leaving it where it is, however. Here, they left the sugar maple as an anchor for the front yard, pruning it to enhance its shape. They widened a pachysandra bed that surrounded the tree by adding plants taken from another bed across the driveway. They also cut back one rhododendron and a euonymus at the corners of the house and transplanted some azaleas, mountain laurel, and mock orange to the backyard. A Korean spice viburnum remained near the front door.

In developing a list of new plants, a landscape architect will study the orientation of the house and the slope of the roof, and check on the balance of light and shade in the yard to see which varieties will thrive where. "Snow and ice build up more readily on the north side of the roof," Nielsin says. "When they slide off, they'll break up most anything planted underneath, especially evergeens." Adds von Trapp, "Shade patterns of outlying trees, even on a neighbor's property, can affect your selection. In fact, every side of the house has its own microclimate." For the Nixons, as for other clients, Wirth chose plants that require little maintenance, mature slowly to a manageable size, and don't need frequent pruning. Some hybridized plants are perfect candidates, especially dwarf varieties, he says, or plants such as yews or spirea, which have been bred to resist disease and pest infestation.

To illustrate how the planting would look, Wirth drew up site plans based on key measurements he took at the house, including the height of the exposed foundation, the height of first-floor windowsills (to be sure no plants would grow to block the windows), and the height and depth of the eaves. As a rule of thumb, short plants should just obscure the foundation, while, in two-story houses, the tallest should rise only to the eaves, to avoid the problem of pruning hard-to-reach limbs in the future. But in this case, Wirth intentionally centered a flowering dogwood called *Cornus kousa* 'Satomi', which branches out like a vase, in the bed near the house. As it matures, it will screen some of the asphalt-shingled roof, "which is more the issue here than the foundation," he says. "This type of dog-

Roger digs up compacted soil to a depth of at least 8 to 12 inches, then grades it away from the house ⅛ inch for every foot to ensure proper rainwater runoff.

Wirth checks the position of a dogwood at the center of the planting area, while Cook prepares the hole for another plant.

This old rhody was transplanted to a new location behind the house. To protect the roots during transport, Roger wrapped the base of the plant in burlap. Once the plant is in its new home, he'll cut branches back so it can grow out in a more graceful shape.

After removing old grass and preparing the newly exposed soil, the crew rolls out new sod for the front lawn. As in the foundation planting bed, the soil receives a heavy dose of nutrients, and sand is added for drainage.

wood also bears a bark that, over time, peels to exhibit several multicolored layers, so it should draw the eye to the entry."

Foundation plantings look much more generous when they are layered. This requires a bed considerably deeper than the traditional linear type. "I like wide and curvy beds," von Trapp says, "because they set off the geometry of the facade of a house." Not only does a curve have "a more natural feel," says Wirth, "but it's also easier to mow around." To extend the design into the yard, Roger planted two "floating" beds, which frame views of the house from the street. One, of pachysandra, encircles the sugar maple. The other, which includes two compact gold sawara cypresses and five spireas, extends from a neighbor's border that incorporates the same types of shrubbery. By repeating the colors, textures, and varieties of plants throughout a bed or yard, Wirth implements a classic method of unifying a landscape design. At the Nixons', white azaleas, dwarf laurel, hellebores, and English yews are clustered throughout the foundation bed, and underplanted with 'Bronze Beauty' ajuga, a hearty ground cover.

Once his clients approved the design, Wirth and Cook made their first trip to the nursery. Some of Wirth's selections had to be modified because the nursery didn't have them in stock. After taking delivery of their choices, The men layed out the plants on their future beds. "It's like paints on a palette," says Wirth. "When they're all there, I compose the picture, adjusting as necessary to achieve a harmonious whole."

PLANTING DETAILS

Cook set aside two full days for the project. He dedicated the first to cleaning out old growth, transplanting healthy specimens to the backyard, pruning trees and shrubs to rid them of dead wood and enhance their shapes, and setting in some of the plants. To ensure that water would drain away from the house, Roger dug out the soil near the foundation and regraded it, making sure to leave a 6-inch-high margin of exposed foundation to encourage ventilation along the rim of the siding; that would discourage mildew and rot from getting a start. Although old soil often settles into a negative grade, which causes water to drain into rather than away from the cellar, the opposite proved true at the Nixon property. "The soil had built up along the foundation and was actually touching the wood siding," Roger says. This made regrading particularly important.

SAXON HOLT (3)

When foundation plantings first go in, they can look very sparse. Because many homeowners want their greenery to look as profuse as possible as quickly as possible, they often err on the side of overcrowding. A foundation plant needs at least three years to mature—and room to spread. Despite their luxuriant appearance, crowded plantings aggravate problems with mildew, rot, and termites, especially when they rub against wood siding. That's why plants should be located at least 18 inches to 2 feet away from the house. One way to help a planting look more lush as it matures is to fill in gaps with annuals or perennials. As the permanent plants fill in, these can be removed or transplanted elsewhere.

Roger rototilled the soil in the beds to loosen it up before digging the holes for individual plants.

This lush entry garden is composed of foundation plants layered in a wide bed, punctuated with colorful perennials.

He also amended the earth with compost to nourish the plants, and added a bit of sand to improve drainage. As he dug the holes, he measured them to the exact depth of each root ball and loosened each plant's roots before setting it in, to help it adjust more quickly. "As I backfill the hole with topsoil, I put the plants two to three inches above grade, so when I smooth out the grade and add mulch, the plants will end up at the correct level," he says. He then watered the soil around each plant to soak the root ball.

On the second day, Roger completed his preparation of the soil, planted the remainder of the beds, and laid new sod where needed in the front yard. "Fresh sod is instant gratification," he says. But it requires work. Roger went in with a sod cutter (see page 29), removed the old grass and weeds,

On this new multi-story home, young trees form the basis for foundation plantings.

rototilled, added compost and sand, and rototilled again. Then he graded, limed, fertilized, and smoothed out the area before laying out the sod strips and watering them.

"New plants are one of the least-expensive investments in your home," says Nielsen. "When you consider how much money people spend on renovating their homes, planting wisely makes a great deal of sense." And the rewards are many, including a house and yard that will be more attractive and make a good impression on anyone who happens by. You hope they'll stop and admire the view. ■

When a house has a raised porch, foundation plantings help to conceal the crawl space area.

Fences,

Paths & Patios

BUILDING BLOCKS FOR OUTDOOR LIVING

A SUCCESSFUL LANDSCAPE IS MORE THAN JUST A HOUSE FRINGED BY greenery. It's a composition, and the role of tying various design elements together often falls to patios, walks, and fences. A patio does this by deception, deliberately blurring the line between outdoors and indoors by making it so easy to enjoy both. A path or walkway stitches the elements together even as it helps you move around in comfort and safety. And like the outline of a drawing, a fence defines borders so you know what's in and what's not. To prevent these features from morphing into maintenance nightmares, choose the right materials and rely only on the most time-tested installation techniques. You'll find out what they are on the following pages.

Laying a Patio of Stone

If durability and low-maintenance are what you're after, it's hard to beat bluestone for an outdoor floor

ITH ALL THE BEAUTY OF A WELL-MANICURED lawn but without the maintenance, a stone patio makes an elegant addition to almost any outdoor living space and will long outlast a wood deck. A variety of flat stones will do—whether they're smooth squares of slate or rough flags of limestone—as long as they can withstand foot traffic and the local climate. for most of his patio projects, *This Old House* landscaping contractor Roger Cook favors 1½- to 2-inch-thick bluestone, a tough, weather-resistant sandstone quarried in New York, Pennsylvania, and Vermont. Although outdoor floors can be made of many other types of stone (see page 102), Roger's advice: select stone that has been quarried nearby. It may be cheaper because of reduced trucking costs, but more importantly, he says, "Local stone just looks right."

"Setting a stone patio is similar to laying bathroom tile," Roger says. As with tile, you prepare a base, level each piece to the next, and fill in the joints. But while most tile can be set with one hand, moving and laying a 2-inch-thick, 100-pound slab of stone takes some brawn and is best handled by two people. "You only want to move them once," Roger says, "so take your time." You can safely "walk" heavy stones into place by resting an edge on the ground and shifting the weight from one corner to the other.

Apart from the pure beauty of a stone patio, Roger offers one other aspect to admire: "The best thing about laying a stone patio is that when you've finished with all the hard work, it's there for good."

MATERIALS
Bluestone comes in rectangles and squares—from 1- to 4-foot-square pieces, in 6-inch increments. Although it is often confused with slate (a smooth, metamorphic rock formed from fine-grained silt), bluestone is actually a grittier, less brittle material derived from sandstone, and traces its lineage back 100 million years. Price depends not only on color, quality, and thickness but also on size. A 1- to 1-½-inch-thick stone measuring 2 by 3 feet costs about $30 in places (about $5 per square foot), but if you live a long way from the Northeast, the shipping expense can easily tack on an extra dollar per square foot.

The stones you choose should have a consistent thickness—

DAVID HAMSLEY

ABOVE: The name bluestone is something of a misnomer, as it includes several different types of sandstone ranging from green, brown, and purple to yellow and blue-gray. The size of the stone and its thickness affect its price. RIGHT: This patio was laid in a random, informal pattern. OPPOSITE: Roger Cook sights through a builder's level to a point on a helper's leveling rod. The level establishes a fixed, horizontal reference plane over the entire job site. By measuring down from that plane, Roger can establish elevations with great accuracy, then duplicate them anywhere.

KINDRA CLINEFF (2)

KINDRA CLINEFF (4)

from 1 to 2 inches—in order to avoid difficulty when setting them. Roger uses only premium stone on patios because of its smooth surface and because it is less likely to fracture during installation. Lower-grade stone is more suited for a rustic-looking stepping-stone walkway than for a patio. Some people prefer a patio with uniform color, but there's no reason not to vary the size and color of the stones to give the patio a quilted, less formal look.

STEP 1: EXCAVATE THE SITE

Mark the work area by driving 3-foot-long wood stakes into the ground about 1 foot outside the corners of the planned patio area.

Set up a builder's level in the middle of the patio area. Find a benchmark—a spot that the surface of the patio will meet and be level with next to the house. Sight through the telescope of the level (photo, previous page) while a helper holds a leveling rod at the benchmark and moves the rod's marker until it falls in the scope's crosshairs. Then, at any stake, have your helper, with the marker still

LEFT: Roger uses a power tamper to compact the base
RIGHT: Starting in one corner, he shovels out enough cement mix to lay one stone at a time.

at the established point on the rod, move the rod up or down until the marker falls in the crosshairs. Mark the stake where it meets the bottom of the rod. Swivel the level and repeat the process at each stake. On the two corner stakes farthest from the house, measure down from the mark $\frac{1}{8}$ inch for every foot between the stakes and the benchmark. This establishes a slight pitch across the patio.

Dig 6 to 12 inches below finish grade to reach the subgrade. Compact the dirt with a power tamper (photo, above left)—you can rent one.

STEP 2: SET THE BASE

Cover the subgrade in layers about 3 inches thick (called lifts) using pack, a blend of $\frac{3}{4}$-inch crushed stone and stone dust. Squirt each lift with a hose to help it settle and to minimize dust. A ton of pack laid 3 inches thick will cover 75 square feet.

Compact each lift with the power tamper. Use a hand tamper close to walls, sidewalks, foundations, or anywhere else the power tamper can't reach. Repeat the process of adding, dampening,

Keeping an eye on his 2-ft. mason's level, Roger taps a slab with a rubber mallet to nuzzle it firmly into the setting bed.

Cutting stone is dusty work and calls for suitable safety gear. To eliminate dust, use a wet-cutting blade cooled with water.

and tamping each 3-inch lift until all the pack is roughly 2½ inches below the marks on the stakes (if you're laying 1½-inch-thick stone).

Drive additional stakes every 2 feet between the corner stakes closest to the house and again on the opposite end of the patio. Stretch a chalk line between the finish grade marks and snap the line against the new stakes. Run strings along the pitch of the patio between the new stakes at their finish-grade marks.

STEP 3: LAY THE STONES

In a wheelbarrow, mix 1 part dry cement with 12 parts stone dust to use as a setting bed for the bluestone. Slowly add enough water to make a stiff mix.

Starting in one corner, shovel out enough mix to lay one stone (photo, above), then level the mixture with a rake or hand trowel. Depending on their size and weight, bluestone slabs will settle

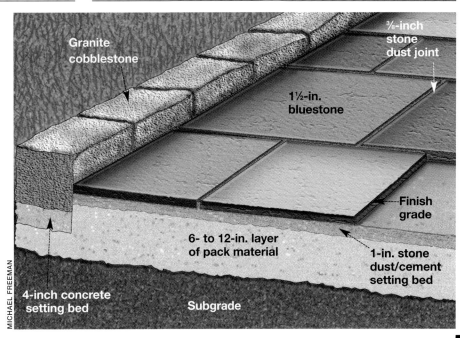

Granite cobblestone

⅜-inch stone dust joint

1½-in. bluestone

Finish grade

6- to 12-in. layer of pack material

1-in. stone dust/cement setting bed

4-inch concrete setting bed

Subgrade

MICHAEL FREEMAN

101

into the wet mix half an inch or more, so spread the mix thicker than its planned final thickness. Check the thickness of the bed by measuring the distance between it and the string. For 1½-inch-thick stones, that distance should be roughly 1 inch, to allow for about half an inch of settling. Add or remove mix to meet the finish grade. One ton of stone dust makes 200 square feet of 1-inch-thick setting bed.

Lower the stone, smoothest face up, into the setting bed. You'll need two people to handle stones weighing 100 pounds or more. Twist the stone slightly to improve its contact with the bed, then tap the slab around the edges and in the center with a rubber mallet (photo, previous page, left). This sets it firmly.

With a level, check the edges of the stone to make sure they are flush with any adjacent slabs, and measure from the strings to make sure the stone is pitched at the correct angle. The face of the stone should be as close to the string as possible without actually touching it. To adjust a stone for flushness and pitch, pry it up with a square shovel, then use a trowel to add or remove wet setting mix.

Repeat the same shoveling, laying, twisting, and tapping procedure for the next stone, leaving a ⅜- to ½-inch gap between stones. Lay a level across both stones to ensure they are in the same plane.

Brush and rinse the stones before the wet mix has a chance to dry. Keep off freshly laid stones for a day or until the setting bed hardens.

STEP 4: CUT STONES TO FIT

Where stones must be cut, scribe a cut-line with a carbide-tipped awl guided by a straightedge (a pencil mark will rub off too easily). Elevate the edge that will be cut off by placing a piece of wood under the cut line (photo, previous page, right). Then put on safety goggles, ear protection, and a dust mask.

To score a slab, use a diamond-grit blade in a circular saw. Set it to a cutting depth of ½ inch and slowly guide the saw along the cut line. Then set the blade to a depth of 1 inch and make one more pass.

Premium-grade bluestone is less likely to flake or chip, so a scoring cut halfway or three-quarters of the way through is sufficient. Just knock off the waste side with a hand sledge. A cheaper, lower-grade stone that's prone to fracturing has to be cut all the way through.

Shallow, even curves can be cut with several tangential and shallow passes. But for tight curves, Roger uses an angle grinder fitted with a 4-inch diamond blade. He makes two passes just as with

LEFT: You'll often find more than bluestone at a stone supplier. Starting from the top: hunter green slate from China; high-desert schist, Southern California; flagstone porphyry, Italy; shell limestone, Texas; and gauged limestone from Indiana.

RIGHT: From the top: pink granite cobblestone, India; Madrid apricot slate, China; Aramosa limestone, Canada; tumbled bluestone, Pennsylvania; and desert gold travertine, New Mexico.

KEVIN REARDON (5)

STONE DUST

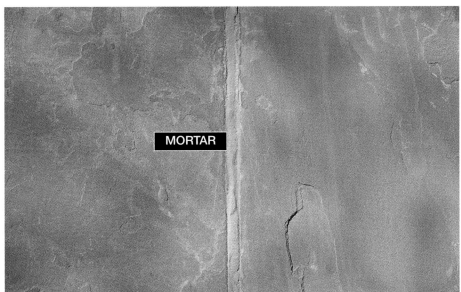

MORTAR

GRASS

the circular saw. Some curves are so tight he has to slice a series of parallel cuts with the circular saw to make small "teeth," then knock them off and smooth the edge with a grinder.

Edging isn't necessary to hold patio stones in place—the setting bed does that—but many people border their patio with cobblestones anyway. To install them, dig a trench far enough into the pack to accommodate a 4-inch bed of concrete and set each stone 4- to 6-inches above finish grade. To keep the stones from toppling backward, Roger tucks a glob of cement behind each one, just enough so it won't be seen beneath the sod.

STEP 5: FILL THE CRACKS

After a day or two, the stones will be solid enough to walk on. But before you can roll out the chaise and enjoy a well-deserved lemonade, you'll have to fill every joint in the patio (photos, left). There are several options here. Roger typically spreads stone dust over the area and sweeps it into the joints. Then he sprays the joints gently with water to encourage the stone dust to pack tightly. A mason's pointing trowel can be used to tamp wet stone dust into the joints. This process is repeated until the joints are firm, evenly filled, and level with the face of the stone.

Mortar creates a solid, low-maintenance joint that foils weeds and ants. But it tends to crack, and it's expensive to install and repair. In cold climates, it may even pop out of the joints. By contrast, loose fillers like stone dust are easy to place and maintain. "Just sweep in more when things settle, about once a year," says veteran mason Roger Hopkins, who has worked stone on many *This Old House* projects. To prevent weeds and washouts, Hopkins mixes one part portland cement into seven parts stone dust, then sweeps the mixture into cracks, packs it with his fingers, and hoses it down lightly. "The cement locks everything together beautifully," says Hopkins, "particularly in a heavily trafficked area. And the portland settles below the surface, so it just looks like stone dust."

Another way to fill joints is with plants. Grass thrives on sunny patios and walks as long as they aren't heavily used. Use stones at least 3 feet across—grass will envelop anything smaller—and leave joints at least 2 or 3 inches wide to keep the roots from drying out. If uneven stones make maneuvering a lawn mower impossible, consider filling in with moss or thyme. Moss grows best in shady areas, where it turn joints into velvety ribbons of green. Sturdy, low-growing thyme produces tiny evergreen leaves, and when you step on it, the scent is irresistible. ■

Building a Paver Walkway

A solid foundation makes any walk sound, no matter what it's made of

THE WALKWAY TO THE FRONT DOOR IS ONE OF THE MOST important features of a home," says Roger Cook, landscaping contractor for *This Old House*. "It's the first thing anyone is going to see." Walkways assembled piece by piece from clay brick or split stone are indeed easy on the eye, but they can be hard on the wallet. Asphalt and poured concrete are more affordable, but these sometimes drab, monotonous surfaces don't always win prizes for appearance. Take that same concrete, however, add mineral pigments and pour the mix into molds, and you have colorful hand-size pavers that mimic the look of cobblestone or brick for about one-quarter the cost.

Unlike asphalt, concrete pavers don't require periodic sealing and don't turn soft in hot weather. And unlike a concrete slab, they won't crack and spall in freezing weather. Other than occasionally sweeping in new sand to replenish the joints, a walk made with pavers needs no maintenance.

Introduced to the United States in the 1970s, all concrete pavers are made of the same basic ingredients: sand, gravel, and portland cement. Mineral pigments impart color, and special additives help prevent damage from freezing weather and de-icing salts. Computer-controlled batching machines measure and blend the dry ingredients with water. The wet concrete is poured into gangs of steel molds, 25 or more at a time, that vibrate while metal plates press down on the mix to squeeze out air pockets. After 15 seconds, the pavers are released from the molds and allowed to cure for 24 hours. The process produces pavers with a compressive strength of at least 8,000 lbs. per square inch, more than twice that of an average house foundation and tough enough to withstand years of harsh weather.

And pavers are a lot easier to install than many other paving possibilities. Roger and his crew spent just two days laying pavers for the 50-foot walkway shown on the facing page. Of course, they brought a full squad of power excavation and compaction equipment to speed things along. "It would take forever with just a rake and a shovel," Roger says. Luckily, all of the gear is readily available at rental centers.

Like old-fashioned cobbles and brick, each paver has to be laid by hand over a carefully leveled bed of sand. "It's not hard to do," Roger says. "In fact, it goes so fast you'll hardly believe it." But before you dig, put some effort into planning.

DAVID CARMACK (2)

Sighting through the telescope of a builder's level allows you to establish key elevations over any length of walkway. Here, Roger Cook takes aim at a distant benchmark.

ABOVE: **Unseen beneath this paver walk are hydronic heating coils.**
LEFT: **Pavers come in a range of shapes, colors, and textures:**
1. Exposed pebble.
2. Octagonal key.
3. Mottled sandstone. 4. Wavy edge.
5. Granite aggregate. 6. Hexagonal.
7. Exposed granite granules.
8. Concrete brick.

KAY BOECKER

PLANNING A WALK

The attributes of a walkway are obvious: It keeps your feet dry and provides safe, easy access to your house. But it can also make the garden more inviting, and connect disparate architectural and landscape elements into a coherent whole.

How well a walk works depends on how well you route it. A *primary* walk leads to or from the front and back doors, and often connects with the street or sidewalk. A walk near the house is often straight to extend the architecture of the building, although this is not a hard-and-fast rule. A straight walk is easy to follow and predictable, and produces a formal look. But you can soften the formality and add interest by planting along its edges.

A *secondary* walk branches off from a primary walk and usually extends farther into the landscape—perhaps to a vegetable garden or secluded bench. Because it doesn't see as much foot traffic as a primary walk, you can make it narrower and less obtrusive. You can also give it gentle curves to make it more casual and level out a gentle climb. One option: Let it follow the dripline of trees (the area that's just outside their branch tips).

The width of a path should relate to its use. A primary walk should be wide enough for two people to walk along side by side. Try to use dimensions that correspond to an architectural feature of your house, such as the combined width of the front door and its trim. That helps to relate path and house to each other.

A secondary walk is more likely to be used by a single walker, and can be narrower—30 to 36 inches wide. Narrower still are casual walks, often called paths, such as a narrow trail of bark mulch that might lead into a wooded area. Varying its width isn't difficult and adds interest.

Be sure walks and paths are wide enough to accommodate outdoor equipment that might run over them. A lawn mower or garden cart, for example, requires about 3 to 4 feet, while a tractor may need 5 feet or more. When in doubt, err on the wide side to ensure that walks are comfortable, safe and easy to follow. Also be sure to position a walk at least an arm's length away from a wall so that walkers won't have to brush against it. That also gives you enough space to include plantings without crowding them.

When you're comfortable with the overall design of your walkway, do your homework. Always call local utility companies to determine the locations of underground gas, electric, cable TV, water, and telephone lines. "Call before you dig" isn't just a catchy slogan—slicing through a live wire can be downright dangerous.

STEP 1: LOCATE THE WALK

On a flat surface, lay out a test row of the pavers to find a pattern and a width that requires you to cut few, if any, pieces along the length of the walk. Cutting pavers is time-consuming. A finished walk should be at least 3½ feet wide, and ideally 5 feet; the exact dimension depends on the pavers.

Using your width dimensions as a guide, mark a rough outline of the walk on the ground using bright spray paint. At each end of the walk, along one side, pound a 2-ft. long wood stake just outside the outline.

Set up the builder's level (photo, page 104) far enough from the work area so it won't be jostled or disturbed. "You absolutely do not want it to move while you're doing this job," Roger says. There are other ways to establish a consistent height across a given area, but there's no better tool than the builder's level. Have a helper hold a leveling rod (see page 99) on a benchmark, the surface that one end of the walkway will meet and be level with. The helper has to move the rod's marker until you see it centered in the crosshairs of the level's telescope. Jot down the elevation of the marker and then repeat the operation at the other end of the walk.

Now have your helper hold the leveling rod against the stake nearest the house. With the marker at the previously determined elevation, have him move the rod until the marker aligns with the level's crosshairs. Swipe a pencil mark where the bottom of the rod now hits the stake: This is the finish elevation of the walkway. Repeat these steps for the stake farthest from the house.

Now tie a length of brightly-colored mason's line between the stakes at the marks.

STEP 2: EXCAVATE

Using the string as a reference, remove dirt to reach rough grade—the depth below the string that equals the total thickness of the pavers, the sand setting bed, and the gravel/stone-dust base (see page 109). "It's okay," says Roger, "to dig a little deeper than necessary, but a base that isn't deep enough will move later on." Depending on the length of the walk, digging is either a job for shovels and lots of time, or a small tractor. The rough-grade excavation should be 16 to 24 inches wider than the finished walkway.

Dig a trench across the rough grade at both ends of the walkway, and place 4-inch-diameter PVC pipe in each trench. The pipes enable irrigation lines or electric wires to be added without disturbing the walk. Cap them with duct tape to keep dirt from getting inside.

Cover the rough grade with a 3- to 4-inch layer of pack (a mix of gravel and stone-dust) and spread with rakes and shovels. Run a plate compactor over the pack to consolidate it.

STEP 3: PACK THE BASE

Pull up the old stakes. At each end of the walk, along one side, pound new stakes just outside the excavation. As in Step 1, use the builder's level and the rod to mark the finish elevation on the stakes. Tie mason's line between them at the marks.

Cover the rough grade with a 3- to 4-inch-thick layer of pack—a mix of gravel and stone-dust—and spread it out with rakes and shovels.

When the pack is fairly even, run a plate compactor over it (photo, above). Also called a power tamper, it mashes the pack into an almost rock-hard layer. Where there's no room to maneuver the compactor, hand-tamp with whatever is handy. Continue adding pack in 3- to 4-inch layers (called lifts), spreading and tamping each layer until the base reaches the subgrade—the level at a distance below the string equal to the thickness of the pavers plus that of the setting bed—here, a total of 3½ inches.

Lay a straight 2×4 over the conduit, and pull it towards you to remove the excess sand. Shovel extra sand into place to fill voids and screed it again.

When the compacting is finished, the base will be as hard and smooth as a sidewalk.

STEP 4: SCREED THE SAND

About every 10 feet, drive new stakes into both sides of the base, just outside where the edges of the finished walkway will be. Mark the stakes on one side of the walk for the finish elevation, as in Steps 1 and 3, but mark the stakes on the other side slightly higher (⅛ inch per foot of walkway width) so the walk will slope and drain water. Along each side of the walk, tie mason's line between the stakes at their marks.

Lay 1-inch-diameter metal conduit (pipe) alongside both sets of the stakes. About every 5 feet, measure the vertical distance from the string to the top of the pipes, which should equal the thickness of a paver plus ¼ inch. Pound the pipes down or add pack underneath them as needed.

Spread sand about an inch deep between the pipes over the length of the walk.

Lay a straight 2×4, called a screed, across both pipes, and pull it to remove the excess sand (left). Fill any low areas with sand and screed again.

A WALK ON THE WARM SIDE

Some homeowners who live where winters are cold will never have to shovel snow or spread rock salt to help visitors reach the house: Their walkways are warmed by an underpaver, hot-water heating system that automatically melts snow and ice.

Heating and plumbing contractor Richard Bilo installs the outdoor portion of such systems as soon as the walkway base has been compacted. First, he lays down 1-inch-thick boards of extruded foam insulation to reduce heat loss to the ground. Then he screws special plastic clips into the foam and snaps 19-mm plastic tubing onto the clips. The polyethylene tubing, spaced in rows 8 inches apart, carries a warm mix of ethylene glycol and water beneath the walkway through one or more loops, depending on the length of the walk.

The tubing is then buried in 1½ inches of sand. The tubes typically pass through holes drilled through the foundation, and are connected to a dedicated heat exchanger in the basement. Bilo says a unit with a heating capacity of 200 Btu per square foot of walkway is enough to handle most of what winter in the Boston area can dish out.

Some heated walks are even smart enough to know when the snow starts flying. A temperature- and moisture-sensitive plate hidden in nearby shrubbery automatically fires up the boiler and turns on the circulating pumps.

Outdoor radiant heating isn't cheap, but some people think enough of it to install it under driveways. Asked if he has such a system at his house, Bilo laughs. "I don't need one. I've got a plow."

Heating and plumbing contractor Richard Bilo installed the outdoor portion of the underpaver, hot-water heating system as soon as Roger finished compacting the base.

ABOVE: Lay the first pavers along the guide string. Work deliberately, because the pavers you lay now will determine the position of many others.

DAVID CARMACK (4)

BELOW: Continue to lay pavers as you fill in the walk. You can kneel on just-laid pavers if you're careful. If the walk incorporates curves, be prepared to spend a lot of time on this detail.

STEP 5: LAY THE PAVERS

Stake guide strings directly above where the outside edges of the walkway will be. Elevation isn't important because the strings are simply a reference mark for keeping the pavers in line. But the strings must be perpendicular to the starting edge (here, the bottom of the front door).

Begin by placing a few pavers against the starting edge and along the line defined by the string (photo, above). Make an L, then fill in between the legs of the L, forming a triangle with a stepped edge. Continue adding pavers until the triangle spans the walkway (photo, right).

Each paver is simply set on the sand against the others—no pounding or fussing necessary. Lugs molded into the side of each paver take the guesswork out of spacing them. "You can lay pavers as fast as you can pick them up," says Roger.

If your walkway incorporates curves, lay the pavers so they extend beyond where you want the finished edge to be. Draw the desired curve on their faces. Then take each paver out and cut along the line using an angle grinder fitted with a 4-inch dia-

mond blade. Put them back in position. "Keep curves to a minimum," Roger advises. "Cutting pavers is slow, difficult, and dusty work." Always wear a dust mask.

STEP 6: EDGE AND TAMP

When all the pavers are in place, remove the conduit and slip the long leg of flexible L-shaped plastic edging under the pavers (photo, left). Walkways made of pavers need edging to hold them in place; otherwise they will loosen up. Secure the edging with 12-inch-long steel spikes. As the spikes rust, they will grow slightly in diameter, helping to hold the edging in place.

Spread about ½ inch of sand on top of the walkway and run the plate compactor over the area twice: once lengthwise, once across. This works the sand into the joints between pavers and compacts the setting bed. Sweep the walk clean, wash it down with a hose to settle the sand into the joints, then invite the neighbors. ▪

LEFT: Slip the long leg of a flexible L-shaped plastic edging under the pavers and drive 12-inch-long steel spikes to secure.

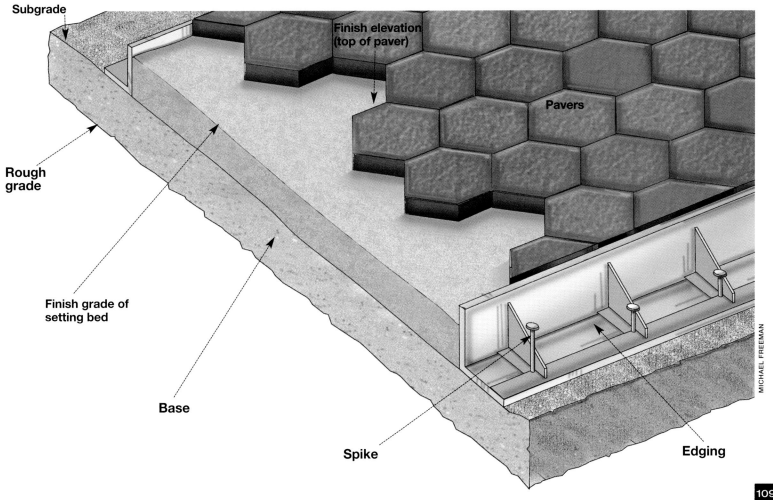

Subgrade

Finish elevation (top of paver)

Pavers

Rough grade

Finish grade of setting bed

Base

Spike

Edging

MICHAEL FREEMAN

Choosing Walk Materials

Safety and durability are prime considerations, but so is versatility

N OT ALL PATHS MUST BE PAVERS. IN FACT, THERE ARE many other surfaces to choose from, including soft surfaces, such as mulches and turf. Hard surfaces, including brick and stone pavers, offer variety as well as good looks.

Consider safety, practicality, appearance, and cost when choosing a surface material. A primary walk that sees heavy traffic must be made from a material that's set firmly in place and provides an even, nonslip surface. Loose, informal materials, like crushed stone or bark, are often inappropriate near an entryway because people track them inside. They're also hard to shovel when it snows, though they're fine for a casual path that leads through a woodland or vegetable garden.

Gravel and crushed stone provide a low-cost, fast-draining surface. These nonslip materials come in a range of colors and sizes, and are also easy to install. Gravel ¾ inch in diameter or smaller is easiest to walk on. Edging is required to keep the stones from traveling, while occasional raking will keep the surface free of leaves and twigs. Gravel is sold in bags and in bulk by the ton or cubic yard. Bulk stones cost less than bagged, but don't forget to account for delivery costs.

Brick can be laid in countless patterns on a walkway. It's relatively affordable, requires little maintenance, and is easy to work with because of its uniform shape. Choose a basic end-on-end pattern, such as running bond or stack bond, for curved walks to avoid extensive brick cutting. And always use paving bricks, not wall bricks. Paving bricks are harder and more durable—especially in cold or wet climates. Wall brick will eventually deteriorate underfoot. For added slip resistance, choose bricks with a rough surface. And as with gravel or pavers, install a stout steel or plastic edging to contain the bricks and prevent them from shifting over time.

STEPPING STONES

Don't hesitate to consider other arrangements besides straight, wide walks if you're after interesting visual illusions. A walk that curves and disappears around a corner, for example, draws attention to what lies beyond. A meandering path can alternately reveal and conceal special plantings, a garden sculpture, or even a striking view. A straight, narrow path can make a garden appear longer, especially if the end point is hidden. On the

Gravel paths are ideal where drainage is a problem. Though the material is easy to install, it must be raked level periodically.

By meandering around obstacles, this brick path creates engaging planting areas on either side.

Informal materials, such as flagstone or even broken concrete, are entirely suitable for garden areas. Wide joints accomodate greenery; narrower joints can be filled with stone dust or sand.

other hand, a curving path or one laid on the diagonal draws the eye from side to side, counteracting an elongated appearance.

Most paths, excluding grass and stepping stones 4 to 5 square feet or larger, require a base of course crushed stone in order to stay level for years to come. Soil type and climate determine how deep to make it—a landscape contractor or stone dealer can provide suggestions for your area. In general, figure on a base 4 inches deep in mild-winter climates with well-drained soil, and 5 to 8 inches deep if you live where the ground freezes.

You can improve drainage in heavy, clay soil by placing a 4-inch-diameter PVC drain pipe down the center of the path, enclosed within the gravel base. Drainage holes in the pipe should face down.

Another way to keep water from pooling on surfaces is to install your path so water drains off. Either install the path so the finished surface is ¼ to ½ inch above the adjacent grade, or slope the path toward one side or the other. The amount of slope shouldn't be noticeable; ¼ inch per foot is generally sufficient. But don't make the common mistake of directing water towards the house foundation or another nearby hard surface—you want it gone, not in your basement.

Apply a leveling course—usually 1 to 2 inches of sand—over the base so you can move a stone or brick around until it's nested just right. A layer of landscape fabric over the gravel base is optional, but it is useful for preventing sand from filtering through the gravel.

OUTDOOR STEPS

Not every walkway meanders along flat ground. When it comes to steps, the choice of stone is critical. Sawn stone is best for uniform steps. Garden steps, however, can be somewhat uneven yet still be safe. "We're more conscious of our footing in a natural setting," says James E. Knode, a landscape architect in Washington. "You don't expect every riser to be exactly six or seven inches high." Depending on the stone and the setting, he recommends that steps be 14 to 16 inches deep, 5 to 7 inches high, and at least 3 feet wide. A single step can be made from several stones, but a single, solid slab is better. Unfortunately, such pieces are usually too heavy to work with. "People buy small stone because it's what they can move," says Bill Hyde, owner of the Marenakos Rock Center in Issaquah, Washington. "But if you go with a stone that's too short in the rise, it feels like you're pitter-pattering. And if the tread's too short, there's no place to land your foot."

Patterned Concrete

With special molds and a bit of imagination, plain old concrete can be made to look like brick, stone, or even tile

THINKING ABOUT CREATING A walk, patio, or even a driveway? You have lots of options. The simplest is ordinary poured concrete: It's affordable and durable, though not very interesting. Or you can invest in the classic beauty of individually laid stones, bricks or pavers. But material costs are high and there's a lot of labor involved.

One paving option that combines the best of both worlds is embossed, or stamped, concrete. This highly convincing trickery starts out as ordinary poured concrete. As the concrete begins to set, realistic-looking stone, brick, tile, or even wood patterns are imprinted onto its surface using textured rubber mats. Special dyes are added to complete the illusion.

Although it costs less than the natural materials it imitates, stamped concrete is still more expensive than plain concrete, according to Kellie Romero, of the Bomanite Corporation, a national franchise based in Madera, California, that claims to have originated the process in 1955. It's also possible to install stamped concrete as a do-it-yourself job; inexpensive plastic molds that form brick and cobblestone patterns are available from various companies. However, for large areas, you might want to opt for the sophisticated stamping patterns and specialized skills of a pro.

To find a concrete contractor who does pattern stamping, check with local masonry yards or contact one of the national companies specializing in these techniques. National companies may train, equip, or even license its contractors as a way of ensuring consistent quality. You'll also find a wide variety of standard patterns and colors, with custom color-matching available. Cost estimates for material and installation are based on the square footage of the job, but extras such as custom patterns and multi-color designs will add to the cost. Steps, curbs, and multiple changes in elevation also increase costs, particularly if they require more labor or special formwork.

One way to cut costs when hiring a pro is to do much of the

ABOVE: To prevent cracking, a patio must be reinforced with steel mesh embedded in the wet concrete.
RIGHT: Flexible rubber embossing mats for the patio were manufactured from molds taken directly from natural stone. This pattern is called ashlar slate.

JOHN NASTA (2)

site-prep work yourself. In the installation shown on the following pages, treated-wood landscape ties were used on the sloping site to frame a network of terraces and landings at multiple levels, including a long run of exterior steps on one side of the house. Areas between these ties were filled later with stamped concrete. Ties were also used for curb borders along the lawn and driveway. All were installed by the homeowner according to specifications provided by the local stamped-concrete contractor. The contractor then came in and poured the concrete, embossed it with a slate pattern, and colored it to create a stonelike appearance.

INSTALLING LANDSCAPE TIES

Building a multilevel arrangement of landscape ties might seem complex, but it's actually a straightforward project that requires few tools and no specialized skills. The following tips will make it even easier:

• Always begin at the lowest point and work upward, especially when dealing with a significant slope. Once the base course is leveled in, it's easy to add steps or change grades.

• A chain saw provides the quickest way to cut 6×6- or 8×8-in. landscape ties, but a circular saw or handsaw will do.

• When using long galvanized spikes to nail the ties together, bore pilot holes with a deep-fluted auger bit to reduce the chance of splitting a tie.

In this project, the ties create interconnected boxes that form the terraces and steps. The completed boxes were backfilled with tamped. free-draining (not loamy) dirt. That was followed by about 4 inches of ¾-inch washed stone topped by about 4 inches of concrete.

If you're doing the work yourself, start by digging a trench equal in depth to two courses of landscape ties. Fill the trench halfway with gravel and add the first tie so its top is even with or slightly above the grade. Check this course with a level, then fill in around both sides with additional gravel. If you're working into a slope, extend the first course into the hill far enough so the end joint and the beginning of the next-higher course are below grade.

As you build courses, be sure to overlap all joints by one-third to one-half the length of each landscape tie (typically 8 feet). Corner joints must also overlap at each course. Secure all corners and intermediate joints with spikes long enough to penetrate the top tie and extend at least halfway through the course below it. Though loosely built, landscape tie walls are susceptible to frost heaves in cold climates due to pressure from groundwater. To keep that from happening, backfill around the ties with stone and bore horizontal holes into the lower courses so water can drain out.

PLACING THE CONCRETE

The landscape tie forms can be filled with concrete as soon as the ties are secure. Ready-mix concrete, ordered by the contractor, must be placed quickly when it arrives. According to Nicole Casal, president of Concrete Images, a 4,000-psi concrete mix typically is used in cold-weather regions to withstand freeze-thaw cycles. This number refers to the strength of the concrete and is a general indication of its watertightness. In milder climates, a 2,500- to 3,000-psi mix should be fine. Pattern stamping begins after the concrete has been leveled (in a process called screeding), and as soon as it's firm enough to be worked. That's usually within an hour or two, depending on the weather and how "wet" the concrete was mixed.

All concrete stamping was once done using heavy, reverse-pattern steel dies mounted on bulky stands or steel drums. These tools were difficult to move around and limited the options of both the contractor and the homeowner. Today, impressions are often done with lightweight, flexible rubber mats. These "skins" can be several feet square and feature continuous, nonrepeating patterns. They can also be cut apart on site to create varying patterns or to fill in hard-to-reach areas.

Unlike the old die patterns, skins don't require an intermediate layer of plastic sheeting to prevent them from sticking to the concrete surface. The contractor first sprays the area with a liquid release agent. Then the skins are placed directly on the concrete and their patterns pounded into the surface with hand tampers. Depending on the desired effect, powdered dyes can be blended into or broadcast atop the concrete at various stages, but always while the concrete is still wet.

In this installation, the contractor returned a few days after the concrete was poured to add a second dye. The concrete surfaces were flooded with water, and then a powdered black colorant was sprinkled over the area. The powder settled into all the creases and crevices creating additional shadow lines, resulting in a surface sure to deceive and delight even the keenest observer. ■

Powdered dye can be broadcast onto the wet concrete to give it color. Chemicals in the dye also accelerate hardening.

The contractor sprays a release agent onto the concrete just before rubber embossing mats are laid over the concrete.

When the mats are in place, one worker pounds on them with a hand tamper to transfer the pattern into the surface of the concrete.

After the concrete hardens, a mason can deepen and define the joints with a wide-blade chisel to imitate the look of hand-laid stone.

JOHN NASTA (4)

Choosing the Best Fence

Here's everything you need to know about siting, style, and picking the best materials for a long-lasting fence

LIFE IMPROVES ON BOTH SIDES OF A FENCE IF YOU choose the right style for the job. Whether you're seeking privacy for your patio, a security wall to keep intruders out, or just the addition of architectural beauty along a property line, the key questions are how much of a visual barrier the fence creates and where it's located. "Tall fences go in the rear, because that's considered private space," says architectural historian Carl Lounsbury, of Colonial Williamsburg and the University of Virginia, in Charlottesville. "Out front, if the house is not immediately on the street, there is that smaller, picket fence that says, 'You're invited to see, but this is my house and my property.'" And whatever fence you choose, remember that your neighbors will be looking at it too. The best guarantee of communal happiness is to discuss the idea with the family on the other side—then share the planning.

Take a quick tour around your community and you'll probably be convinced that there's no one type of fence that suits every situation. But no matter how unusual the design, all fences consist of the same basic elements: posts set into the ground, two or more horizontal rails that are fastened to the posts, and the fencing itself, which is attached to the rails. Posts are generally no more than 6 feet to 8 feet apart for a very practical reason: any farther and the rails are likely to sag.

A building permit isn't usually required to build a fence. But because codes vary from town to town, check with your local building department just to be certain. Also ask about any requirements for materials, picket spacing, setback distances from property lines, and posthole footings.

POSITIONING A FENCE

With apologies to Robert Frost, boundary expert Walter Robillard says that "Good fences—on the proper line—make good neighbors." Boundary disputes are common, although only about 1,000 cases wind up in American courtrooms every year, by Robillard's estimates. "But these disputes are charged with emotion precisely because they are between neighbors," he says, adding that most bordar disputes concern differences of less than five feet. Robillard, a surveyor, attorney, and coauthor of *Brown's Boundary Control and Legal Principles*, says the position of a fence is governed by state property-rights laws, and

REDWOOD · MAHOGANY · WHITE CEDAR · PRESSURE-TREATED PINE · BAMBOO · RED CEDAR

KAY BOECKER

Not every picket behaves the same when put on a fence, where it will be baked by the sun and battered by the elements. The best choices are stable and naturally rot- and insect-resistant woods, such as cedar, mahogany, and redwood. Pressure-treated pine is cheaper and just as durable, but requires extra attention to prevent it from twisting and cracking. Bamboo is somewhat less durable.

JOHN KERNICK

those vary somewhat from location to location. In general, however, he recommends positioning your fence (including concrete for the posts, if you use it) so that it's an inch or two within your property line (as described by a survey). That way, he says, "you have total control over it." But don't leave too much of your plot on the other side of your fence, he cautions, because over the years fences can become the boundary "by estoppel"—applied to fences, the legal phrase means that a fence that leads others to believe it represents the true boundary between properties *becomes* the true boundary.

Robillard says that replacing an existing fence on the same location, however, is generally a safe bet because you're maintaining the history of an accepted boundary. If you're putting up a fence for the first time and aren't sure of your boundary, hire a licensed surveyor to find it based on town records. If you build a fence and your neighbor says it's on his land, ask to see his survey. "Surveyors are like doctors," says Robillard. "They can have different opinions." When differing opinions can't be resolved, though, that's when people end up in court.

FENCES WITH PURPOSE

The design of a fence can be as imaginative or traditional as its owner wants, but most any fence will fulfill at least one of three basic purposes.

Screening fences are designed to cloak eyesores or create privacy, but that doesn't mean they have to be solid, wall-like barriers. Small openings—between louvers or within latticework, for instance—provide air flow, a modicum of visibility, and an appealing look.

Boundary fences identify territory. A 3- to 4-foot-high fence is good for drawing a border around your property without blocking the view. The most common versions are rail fences, reminiscent of horse pastures, and classic pickets, which can keep a small dog in the yard as well as discourage other dogs—and people—from entry.

Security fences safeguard a property, and to do this they need particular characteristics. A security fence should be 6 to 8 feet tall, offer no footholds on the outside, and have a thin top edge or sharp pickets that make it difficult to grab. Some towns limit the height of fences, so check with the local zoning department before you get too carried away with your stockade. And if the main job of the fence is to enclose a swimming pool, make sure to consult town ordinances—and your insurance company—for specific design requirements.

MICHAEL FREEMAN (9)

STYLE: Alternating slat
PURPOSE: Screening

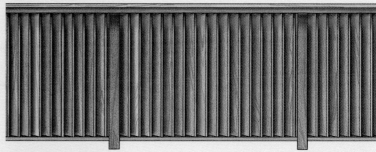

STYLE: Vertical louver
PURPOSE: Screening

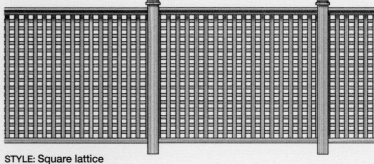

STYLE: Square lattice
PURPOSE: Screening

STYLE: Square lattice over diagonal lattice
PURPOSE: Screening

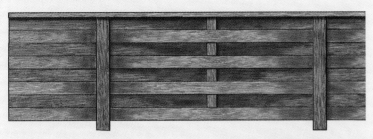

STYLE: Horizontal basket weave
PURPOSE: Screening

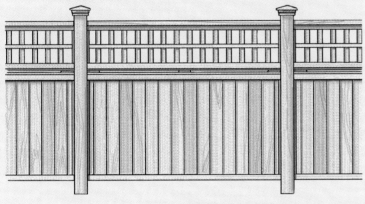

STYLE: Board with large-lattice topper
PURPOSE: Screening

STYLE: Tulip-top picket
PURPOSE: Boundary

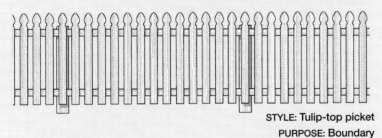

STYLE: Three-rail
PURPOSE: Boundary

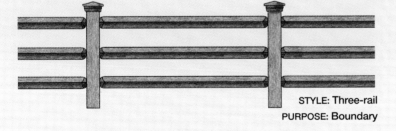

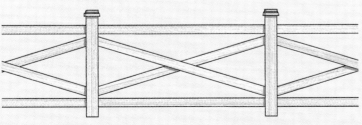

STYLE: Kentucky Derby-style
PURPOSE: Boundary

CHOOSING THE RIGHT WOOD

Because fences bear the brunt of the elements, only the toughest woods will survive. Roger Cook, *This Old House* landscape contractor, says that naturally rot- and insect-resistant cedar, mahogany, and redwood will last 15 to 25 years above ground, and 10 to 15 years as posts. Pressure-treated pine is cheaper and just as durable, but Roger warns that it may warp and crack over time. Bamboo offers an Asian flavor but survives only about 15 years.

Redwood and cedar (both western red cedar and eastern white cedar) make beautiful fences, and the heartwood is resistant to disease and insects. At least one of these species will be available in most regions, although heartwood grades may have to be special ordered.

When choosing cedar, use only heartwood—the sapwood is more susceptible to rot. As for redwood, the grades are a little more complicated. Fencing boards should be made from Construction Heart, Construction Common, Merchantable Heart, or Merchantable grades. For greater durability, posts and any other element that will touch the ground should be made from Clear All Heart, Select Heart, Construction Heart, or Merchantable Heart grades.

Preservative-treated wood has been the most economical choice for wood fences. This material is typically southern yellow pine infused with a preservative called chromated copper arsenate (CCA). However, this chemical will no longer be available for residential use after December 2003, due to phaseout mandated by the Environmental Protection Agency. Other preservatives will be available, however.

Preservative-treated pine can last more than 50 years in the ground, but unfortunately it's prone to twisting, checking, and other flaws that crop up as the wood dries out. These problems can be controlled by treating the fence with a water repellent, or with a stain that contains one. Unless the wood is kiln-dried after treatment (KDAT), you'll have to wait about six months before applying a water repellent. For a fence installed in the summer in northern climates, that could mean a year's exposure to the elements.

The durability of treated wood increases with the amount of chemicals in the wood, notes Roger. For in-ground posts, look for pressure-treated wood rated for in-ground contact. That means it will have a chemical retention of 0.40 lbs./cu. ft. instead of a lighter-duty 0.29 lbs./cu. ft.

Though no wood resists rot and insects as well as pressure-treated products, not everyone likes the look of treated wood. With some fences, though, you can have it both ways by installing treated posts to support fencing of a more attractive wood. Some people use pressure-treated wood for posts and a warp-resistant species such as spruce for the fencing; 8-foot sections of prefab spruce fencing sell for less than $20 at home centers. However, spruce doesn't age as well as cedar, lasting perhaps five to eight years, so money you save in the short term will be spent later on painting, staining, or replacing pickets.

A FENCE THAT'S NOT WOOD

Wood is nearly everyone's favorite fencing material, but in recent years vinyl has become a viable option. Vinyl fences are available in a wide range of styles, and they even come in such colors as white, tan, and gray. Depending on the product, posts and support rails may be reinforced with galvanized-steel inserts. Because vinyl fencing is made using a process where plastic is extruded through a mold, the easy-to-create shapes are less expensive than if they were rendered in wood. Of course, the real appeal of vinyl is that it reduces maintenance chores—some products are guaranteed for 20 years against peeling, flaking, rusting, blisters, and corrosion. What's more, most vinyl fences look identical from either side.

One drawback of vinyl is that it can become brittle with age and in cold weather, and it can fade in strong sun. Look for products that contain UV inhibitors to counter this tendency. Virgin vinyl is a better material than recycled vinyl because of its purity. Vinyl that has been factory-treated with an impact modifier is generally less likely than other vinyls to shatter or crack.

PROTECTING POSTS

All wood fences consist of vertical posts connected by horizontal rails (pickets and filler boards are optional). But it's the posts, sitting in moist, fungi-rich earth, that decay the fastest. Setting them in concrete is little help—it holds water against the wood—so Roger uses gravel, which drains the water away. He digs a hole deep enough to bury a third of the post's length and 2 to 4 inches wider than the post to give himself room to level and align it. Then he tamps the bottom of the hole, shovels in about 6 inches of gravel, and inserts the post. As he fills the hole with gravel, he tamps around the post and repeatedly checks it for plumb.

Roger fastens rails to posts with hot-dipped galvanized nails, and attaches pickets to rails with stainless-steel ring-shank nails, which hold better

MICHAEL FREEMAN (9)

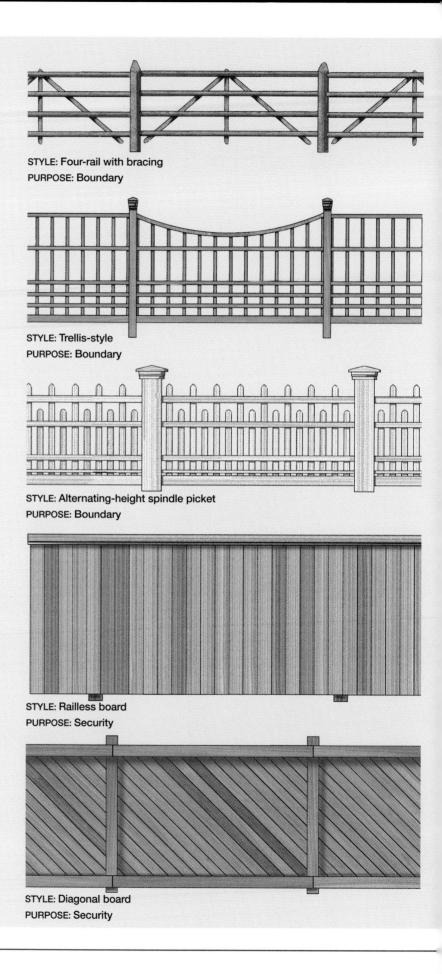

STYLE: Four-rail with bracing
PURPOSE: Boundary

STYLE: Trellis-style
PURPOSE: Boundary

STYLE: Alternating-height spindle picket
PURPOSE: Boundary

STYLE: Railless board
PURPOSE: Security

STYLE: Diagonal board
PURPOSE: Security

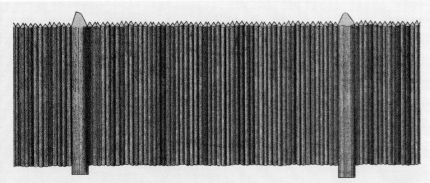

STYLE: Rustic stockade
PURPOSE: Security

STYLE: Sawtooth board
PURPOSE: Security

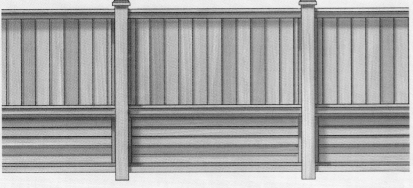

STYLE: Vertical board over horizontal board
PURPOSE: Security

STYLE: Vertical board with urn finials
PURPOSE: Security

stainless-steel ring-shank nails, which hold better than the smooth-shank variety. Nails made of unprotected steel are cheaper, but they quickly corrode and streak the wood with tracks of rust.

Try to work post caps into your fence design. They add more than a decorative touch: A solid cap, whether wood or metal, sheds water that would otherwise soak into the vulnerable end grain of the post. If you skip the cap, you can give exposed post ends some protection by coating them with wood preservative, but it's really not the best way to go. Roger says that protecting posts with a solid cap can give them five more years of life, depending on climatic and soil conditions. Preformed metal or wood caps can be found wherever fence materials are sold. If you don't want caps, at least cut the post tops to encourage water to drain way. An angle of 15° is about right.

Some fence designs call for the rails to be "let in" to the posts. This means wide, horizontal notches have to be cut in the side of the posts. Rails fit into the notches. This gives the rails extra support and allows them to fit closer to the centerline of the post for a cleaner look. But if taking the trouble to cut all those notches, be sure you don't reduce the durability of your fence at the same time. Water that gets into the joints can play havoc with any areas of exposed end grain on the post. To minimize this problem, brush a clear wood preservative over the notched areas. Be sure to check labels to make sure the preservative is compatible with any other finish you plan to use on your fence.

FENCE FINISHES

Painted fences are charming but require scraping and repainting every five years or so, says Roger. And if the paint film isn't constantly touched up, water that reaches the wood will encourage rot. If you insist on paint, prime the bare wood first, then apply the best-quality paint you can afford.

Opaque stains don't last as long as paint, but they demand less prep work when it's time for a new coat. Semitransparent stains are the easiest to apply and maintain because they soak into the wood instead of creating a hard film on the outside. Instead of peeling, they just fade away in three to five years, so no scraping is required to prep the surface. And whenever you want the fence to look its best, just brush more on—as long as the surface is clean, you won't have to sand or scrape it.

But when it comes to fence finishing, Roger prefers the simplest option: leaving the wood untreated. "It weathers to a gray that blends in with the landscape," he says.

Proper Picket

A fence with square pickets, installed in sections, keeps young kids safe

JOHN AND ALISON CARIATI LOVE THE TIMEWORN features of their 1817 clapboard-covered house in Hingham, Massachusetts: the floors canting toward the back wall, the door latches rubbed smooth from generations of use, the exposed beams clearly hewn by hand. But the aging fence that surrounded the property when the Cariatis purchased it wasn't so charming. "The pickets were completely rotten," says Alison, and the eyesore didn't even function as a barrier. With a busy street just 15 feet in front of the house and two young children in the family, the Cariatis knew they would have to make replacing the fence a priority.

From small towns to large cities, suburban neighborhoods to rolling fields, picket fences are a quintessential part of the American landscape. The wood barriers are direct descendants of sharpened-log stockades built by settlers to fortify frontier encampments. Over time, as the dangers of the wilderness

ABOVE: A portion of the backyard board fence is topped with spindles that match the picket fence.
RIGHT: A Boston digger scoops soil out of a narrow posthole.

receded, fences became shorter and more refined, and were erected mostly to contain livestock and establish property lines. By the early 19th century, when the Cariatis' home was built, the picket fence was widely used as a decorative border for residential yards.

SHOPPING FOR A DESIGN

Today's busy streets and small building lots make fences more practical then ever. In addition to defining property borders and screening out undesirable views, a fence can make a small front yard look bigger by separating it from the street. Or it can make a house the focal point of a big lawn by establishing a frame around it. And from a practical standpoint, a fence can keep kids and dogs in, eliminate casual shortcutting, and discourage crimes of opportunity.

A well-built, well-styled, and well-maintained fence will enhance the appearance of a house by providing a visual accent. Similarly, one that's inappropriate or falling apart can mar the look of an entire street—which is one reason why many communities regulate height (and why homeowners should always check with the zoning department when planning a fence installation). Hingham, a historic suburb of Boston, goes a step further: The Cariatis' fence design needed approval from the Historic Districts Commission. But first Alison and John had to pick a design.

"The choices were a little overwhelming," says Alison. She knew she wanted a picket fence, but that still left a daunting number of options. Pickets can be flat or square, with pointed, rounded, or arched tips. Posts can be smooth or fluted, with any number of decorative caps. Pickets can even be topped with a cap rail, and the outside face dressed up with a fascia and kickboard (horizontal boards corresponding to the inside top and bottom rails). The Cariatis also had to select the picket height, which typically runs between 3 and 6 feet, and decide if the tops of each section would be straight, scalloped, arched, or staggered. And finally, they had to consider the width of the pickets and the amount of space between them.

The couple scouted for ideas by strolling through town. They also scoured catalogs from fence manufacturers, eventually settling on Walpole Woodworkers as their contractor. By the time Walpole design consultant Ron Brown arrived at their house with picket samples, the Cariatis had a pretty good idea of what they wanted.

Thy decided on a $1\frac{5}{8}$-inch square picket, in a straight-topped shape, accented by fascias and kickboards. "We discussed a flat picket, but when

I got my hands on that square sample, I knew it was the one," says John. "It's much sturdier." The couple had intended to order 3-foot-high pickets (the same height as the existing fence), but Brown convinced them that a 3½-foot height would screen out a little more of the busy street without appearing overly intimidating. The backyard would be enclosed with a 6-foot-high solid-board privacy fence topped with decorative spindles. The Cariatis presented a catalog clipping of their proposed fence at a Historic Districts Commission hearing, and the plans were approved.

Walpole made the choice of wood easy for the Cariatis: The company uses only northern white cedar, which is naturally rot and insect resistant.

LEFT: Details such as curved rails and decorative post caps set the tone for this classic fence.
BELOW: Each 8-foot-long fence section has extra-long rails that slide into mortises cut into the posts.

Cedar is expensive: High demand and dwindling supply have driven the wholesale price up more than 50 percent in the last five years or so, says Peter Lammert, a forester for the state of Maine. Including the backyard privacy screen, the Cariatis paid about $60 per installed foot for their fencing, a price that included removal of the old fence. Mark Bushway, regional sales manager for Walpole, says that's at the high end of their picket fence line; a rustic picket fence with simple round posts could run as low as $20 per foot installed. In other parts of the country, western red cedar, redwood, cypress, and even mahogany offer similar durability at comparable prices. Picket fences can be built more inexpensively still by using pressure-treated lumber.

Pickets should be fastened to rails using high-quality galvanized nails. Make sure they're hot dipped; electroplate galvanizing is too thin and can wear off, causing nails to rust. Stainless-steel nails generally aren't worth their extra cost because the fence itself won't last as long as they do.

Picket fences were once installed one board at a time on the job site, and that's still the way most do-it-yourselfers tackle it. Fence companies, though, prefabricate 8-foot-long sections in the controlled environment of a shop. Some companies even put a finish on the sections at the factory, which can save time and money compared with painting or staining on site. Walpole applies a latex solid-color stain to fence sections, flow-coating the liquid into every crack. Stain is thinner and less durable than paint, but it won't peel or chip, and it's easier to reapply.

Cedar weathers to an appealing gray if left unpainted, although it should still be treated every two years with a linseed oil–based preservative. Pressure-treated wood has a greenish hue that makes it unsuitable for a natural finish. The green will disappear under a coat of oil-based paint or solid stain, but the wood should be allowed to weather for a year first.

INSTALLING THE FENCE

Many homeowners leave fence installation to skilled pros like veteran Walpole foreman Joe Orem, who built the Cariati fence. Orem and a helper, Jeremiah Brow, pulled up to the Cariatis' on a clear, crisp spring day with a truckload of posts and fence sections. First, however, they had to remove the old fence; since its posts were anchored in concrete, out came the sledgehammer.

Concrete is the subject of considerable controversy in the fence trade. Some builders swear by it, citing its undeniable strength for setting posts;

but Orem cautions that as the wood shrinks, small gaps form between the post and the concrete, allowing destructive moisture to pool around the wood. (By contrast, water drains away from posts set in backfill or gravel.) And, as Orem points out with a sigh, concrete makes fence removal hard. He only uses it for gateposts, which are subject to more stress and movement, and in situations where holes cannot be dug deep enough for conventional backfill.

With the old fence out of the way, Orem made sure no utility lines ran beneath the site, then dug the first posthole at the street corner nearest the driveway. Surprisingly enough, pros in these parts don't use power diggers; the spinning auger blades are no match for New England's famously rocky soil. Orem prefers a lever-action tool called a Boston digger (photo, page 122). It's better than the standard clamshell digger, which is only good to a depth of 2 feet before the hole itself blocks the handles from spreading. The Boston digger operates differently, with a lever at the top which operates a small scoop at the bottom. It can dig 3½ feet down before the mechanism gets in the way. Boulders are still removed the old-fashioned way: with sweat and long iron bars.

How deep is deep enough for setting posts? That depends on the climate (thawing and freezing of the earth is what causes posts to heave out of the ground) and the condition of the soil. In frost-free zones with reasonably firm soil, 2 feet is sufficient. In Massachusetts, 3 feet is the minimum—and deeper is better. Agricultural engineers calculate that every 6 additional inches of depth doubles a post's resistance to pullout.

With the first of their 3-foot holes ready, Orem and Brow hefted a 7-foot-long post into it, backfilling with the removed soil and using a level to make sure the post was plumb. (Plain posts can go in longer than needed and be cut to even height later, but intricate posts like these must be carefully set to height in the hole.) Then, to establish a straight line, Orem ran a mason's line down to the next post position, dropped a plumb bob from the line to locate the next hole, and dug again. Both ends of the rails from each picket section fit into factory-cut mortises in the posts, so he and Brow had to simultaneously jockey the position of the second post and slip in the first section to secure a fit. "You can't go around and put in all the posts first," he says, "because you'll never be able to wiggle the sections in."

Orem had to follow the curve of an existing stone footing that runs along the front of the property under the fence, while maintaining a level

CRAIG RAINE (2)

ABOVE: As a finishing touch, fascias and kickboards were nailed to the pickets.
RIGHT: Fence installer Joe Orem uses scrap 4×4 blocks to suport the gate as he screws strap hinges into place. The X-shaped bracing prevents the gate from sagging.

fence over ground that was anything but. He also had to balance the desire to keep an even line of pickets with the need to follow the natural contour of the yard. It boiled down to old-fashioned eyeballing, which comes from experience.

"The fence went up pretty well," says Orem, "until we hit that ledge by the driveway." Ledge—a layer of solid rock at or near ground level—is a fencebuilder's nightmare. Sometimes special pins can be drilled into the ledge and fastened with fast-drying hydraulic cement. But at the Cariatis', says Orem, "we just kinda hammered away at it with the digging bars and were able to get the posts down far enough to anchor with concrete." After the fence was assembled, Orem drove 3½-inch nails into each mortise-and-tenon joint for extra strength, then nailed on the fascias and kickboard.

Finally, Orem installed the gates, placing the gate bolts too high for the kids to reach. Now son Amos, 5, and daughter Hannah, 2, can frolic happily in the confines of their yard, protected from traffic. "We don't have to worry about their safety," says John, "and the place looks great." ■

Building A Gate

Outdoor woodwork that's welcoming

SPRING, WITH ITS WARM WEATHER AND LENGTHENING days, marks the unofficial start of the outdoor building season. But if you escaped being bitten by the springtime building bug, here's a project sure to get you outdoors with your tools. If you're looking for something a bit less ambitious than a deck or shed, consider a gate. This simple-yet-stately project can be completed in about three days for less than $300.

The gate shown here features fluted posts, dentil molding, turned finials, and elegant pickets graced with an eyebrow top. The gate tucks neatly between two hedges that border a sidewalk. But its classic styling and universal appeal would look just as handsome at the entrance to a garden, in a fence line, or straddling a brick walkway.

Durable exterior-grade materials ward off rot and rust. The two posts are pressure-treated 6×6s wrapped with red cedar 1×8s, but only the pressure-treated stock extends into the earth. The gate itself is made entirely of red cedar 1×4s. And the entire assembly relies on galvanized nails and hardware.

Spacing the ten pickets ¾ in. apart made the gate a comfortable 41¾ inches wide—more than enough for a wheelbarrow, push mower, or hand truck. The cedar-clad posts are 42½ inches apart, leaving ⅜ inches of clearance on each side of the gate.

If that spacing is tight, though, the posts can be set closer together to support a 36- or 30-inch-wide gate. They can also be spaced farther apart for a gate 48 inches wide. Spread them any farther, though, and you'll have to build two swinging gate sections and hang one off each post. If you expect to move a garden tractor or large riding mower through the gate, this is an option you ought to consider.

SETTING THE POSTS

The first step is to dig the two postholes using a posthole digger or power auger. Each hole must be at least 12 inches in diameter and about 24 inches deep. Line the hole bottoms with 2 inches of gravel for proper drainage. Then set the posts in the holes, leaving 41 in. sticking above the ground. Try this work-saving tip: Buy a 12-ft. long 6×6 and have the lumberyard saw it into two 63-inch-long posts. That eliminates the need to cut the big posts on site.

Align the posts with each other, then plumb them with a

This Victorian-inspired gate features an eyebrow top, fluted posts, dentil molding, and turned wood finials.

JOHN DECKER (3)

TOP: The uncut ends of the posts should go in the ground. Set the posts by adding water to each hole and shoveling in dry concrete mix.

ABOVE: Cut flutes into the cedar trim boards with a router guided by an adjustable router fence.

level. Hold the posts in position temporarily with wood braces and stakes and set the posts in concrete. Some people prefer standard concrete and mix it in a wheelbarrow, but there's a faster method for postholes. Fill the holes halfway with water, shovel in dry fast-setting concrete (photo 1) and mix thoroughly. If necessary, add more water, but don't let the mix get soupy. You'll need two 60-lb. sacks of concrete mix for each hole. That may seem like a lot, but it really isn't—you'll be

Fasten the fluted trim boards to the posts with galvanized finishing nails.

Trim the posts with dentil molding. Cut the pieces to form miter joints and fasten them with 1½-inch-long finishing nails.

surprised at how much mix those holes gobble up. Besides, concrete mix isn't expensive. Allow the concrete to stiffen overnight or longer before you remove the braces.

TRIMMING OUT THE POSTS

To make the decorative cladding for the posts, start by cutting eight 41-inch-long pieces of 1×8 cedar. Rip four of the boards down to a width of 5½ inches and nail them to the left and right sides of the posts with 8d galvanized finishing nails.

Rip the remaining four pieces down to 7 inches wide to cover the fronts and backs of the posts. You'll need to rout five decorative flutes into each of the boards before nailing them in place, however. Use a router fitted with a ⅝-inch-diameter core-box bit. Set the tool to make a ⅜-inch-deep cut and attach a router fence (edge guide) to its base. Clamp the cedar 1×8 to a workbench, then clamp a narrow wood strip across each end as a starting and stopping point for the router. Position these strips so the flutes begin and end about 3½ inches from each end of the board. Then adjust the router fence so that its face is 3½ inches from the centerline of the bit.

Rout the middle flute, readjust the fence so that it's 1 inch closer to the bit, then rout the second flute. Move around to the other side of the board and rout the third flute. Slide in the fence another inch and rout the final two flutes, one from each side (photo 2, previous page). Repeat this sequence for the remaining 1×8s. Smooth

Mark the shingle molding to length while holding it in place to avoid any measuring mistakes.

JOHN DECKER (6)

Apply a circle of water-resistant glue onto the top of the beveled post cap before screwing on the finial.

After gluing and clamping the gate parts together, nail through the 1×4 bracing and into the back of the pickets.

Cut the graceful curve along the top of the gate with a saber saw fitted with a fine-tooth blade.

each board with 120-grit sandpaper. Then nail the fluted boards to the fronts and backs of the posts using 8d finishing nails (photo 3).

The top of each post incorporates dentil molding, shingle molding, a post cap, and a finial. Fasten the dentil pieces with 4d galvanized finishing nails (photo 4). Then nail a 1×8 filler block to the top of the post so it covers all four pieces of the dentil molding. Nail 1⅛-in. shingle molding to the edge of the block so that the pieces overlap the dentil molding slightly (photo 5); miter-cut the pieces and attach them with 4d finishing nails.

You can buy beveled post caps, but why not make them? Start by gluing and clamping together three 24-inch-long pieces of 1×12 cedar; be sure to use a water-resistant adhesive. After the glue has dried, saw the laminated blank into two 11-inch-square blocks. The easiest way to bevel-cut each cap is on a table saw with the blade tilted to 15 degrees, though a band saw also works. Next, smooth the bottom edges of each beveled cap with a ½-inch rounding-over bit. Then nail the caps to the tops of the posts with 10d finishing nails.

To attach the finials, bore a ¼-inch-diameter hole 1 inch deep into the center of each cap and encircle it with a continuous bead of water-resistant glue. Then mount each finial using a ⅜-inch-diameter double-ended lag screw (photo 6).

BUILDING THE GATE

The gate consists of 41½-inch-tall 1×4 pickets held together by 1×4 braces glued and nailed in a Z-pattern across the back. When fastening the 1×4 braces, place a ¾-inch block between each picket to maintain consistent spacing (photo 7).

To form the graceful eyebrow curve at the top of the gate, start by drawing half of the shape onto heavy paper or thin cardboard. Cut out the drawing and trace it onto half of the gate. Then flip the pattern over, trace the other half, and cut the curve using a saber saw fitted with a fine-tooth blade (photo 8).

Set all nails and fill the holes with exterior-grade wood putty. Then paint or stain the gate and posts.

HANGING THE GATE

Stand the gate between the posts and use shims to center it in the opening. Place blocks beneath to keep it at least 2 inches off the ground. With the shims and blocks holding the gate securely in position, screw the hinges to the post and gate. Check that the gate swings freely, then install the latch.

Nail a small cedar stop block to the inside of the post just blow the latch to keep the gate from swinging the wrong way. Then stand back and admire your work.

Outbuilding

S, Porches & Decks

OUTDOOR AMENITIES FOR ANY LIFESTYLE

HAVE YOU BEEN DREAMING OF WAYS TO MAXIMIZE your time outdoors? If so, you'll want to read this chapter to find a wealth of ideas for stylish outbuildings, versatile decks, and cool, bug-free screened porches. You'll learn Tom Silva's secrets for picking lumber, and find out about recent developments that dramatically change the type of decking materials you should consider. You'll also find our guide to the essentials of deck construction, from installing footings to choosing—and maintaining—finishes.

Building Small Scale

Storage shed or studio, a little building puts imagination into the landscape

THERE'S NO DENYING IT: HOMEOWNERS COLLECT STUFF. Lots of stuff. They cram it into the crawl space, box it up in the basement, and stack great cardboard pillars of stuff in the garage. But finding a place for everything, and everything in its place, is practically impossible once you add the unwieldy accoutrements of modern life such as lawn mower, bikes, ladders, snow tires, garden tiller, lumber, lawn furniture, hose reels, sleds. . . And it doesn't stop there. Increasingly, homeowners also need a private place to indulge in their passions, whether it's potting plants, writing screenplays, or carving ducks.

What's needed is a home away from home, whether you call it a shed, an outbuilding, or a backyard studio. Though just about any homeowner with basic carpentry skills and a modest collection of tools can build something serviceable, the challenge is keeping whatever you build from looking like a wart on the landscape. Most of the metal storage buildings and prefabricated wood buildings sold at home centers and garden shops are strictly utilitarian, and maybe even ugly. Although their low prices are enticing, with few exceptions, these basic buildings get uglier over time as they're exposed to the elements.

Fortunately, small buildings can be functional and good looking as well as durable. There are three common ways to tackle the construction: order a set of plans and build from scratch; buy a ready-to-assemble kit; or hire a contractor who specializes in small buildings. You'll find such contractors in the yellow pages under "Tool & Utility Sheds," "Storage Buildings," or "Garage Builders."

Building from plans is the least-expensive option. Of course, it also entails the most work and time. Mail-order outbuilding plans typically cost $20 to $30, and are often available from companies that sell home plans. Local shed contractors are another possible source of plans, though most prefer to sell the complete structure. And you can often find free or low-cost plans at major lumber suppliers, or in publications from various trade associations that promote the use of lumber.

Not up to building from scratch? Then consider a ready-to-assemble (RTA) building. These kits are an appealing compromise between economy and ease of construction. Their

ABOVE: Gingerbread screwed to the gable-end rafters of this backyard photo studio was cut with a jigsaw; sharp edges were rounded with a router.
RIGHT: Old doors were sawed in half lengthwise to make the shutters.

MATTHEW BENSON

preassembled panels go together like a jigsaw puzzle. And all the parts are precut, so there's nothing to saw—even the doors are prehung. In most cases, two people can put up an appealing 8×8-foot building in a single day.

There are hundreds of small RTA companies across the country, though they don't always have a wide selection of designs. When buying one, be

This 12×12-foot retreat was built from stock plans. The Japenese-inspired details create a structure that's rustic, yet refined.

sure to ask what you'll have to provide. Usually, you must supply the roof shingles, floor framing, and paint or stain. Whether they're included or not, the floor framing and support posts should be pressure-treated wood rated for ground contact, which offers optimum protection from rot and wood-boring bugs. Pay particular attention to hardware and fasteners. All metal parts, including door hardware, should be made of either hot-dipped galvanized metal (which is inexpensive and widely available) or stainless steel (harder to find, and more expensive, but much longer lasting).

The easiest way to get an outbuilding built is to hire a local contractor. Of course, this is also the most expensive option—figure on $2,000 to $3,000 for a basic 10×10-foot structure. But this option does provide the greatest design flexibility, because most contractors will alter an existing design or custom-build one to suit your site as well as your particular requirements. What's more, a contractor often can install even a fairly large shell in one day by preassembling some of the components in the workshop.

Contractors who specialize in this work typically have models available for you to view. Visit them, and use a tape measure to make sure the doorway is wide enough and the ceiling tall enough to suit your storage needs. If models aren't available, ask for the names of former clients and try to arrange a visit to their outbuildings.

WORTHWHILE FEATURES

Whether you decide to use a plan or a ready-to-assemble kit or hire a contractor, give some thought to the details that will match your building to your needs. Consider adding one or more of the following accessories to your project:

• A ramp, especially if you plan to store a mower, tractor, bicycles, or a motorcycle;

• Enlarged doorways, required for driving in tractors and riding mowers;

This 1803 summer kitchen was dismantled, moved, then restored. It now serves as a backyard retreat for dinners cooked on its open-hearth fireplace.

MATTHEW BENSON

BELOW: Exterior walls of the building at left were framed, sided, and then slid into place within the log frame.

• Built-in shelving to help keep tools and supplies neatly organized;

• A loft for extra storage in the "attic" area;

• An easily-cleaned workbench, particularly useful in a greenhouse or potting shed;

• A skylight to brighten the interior, and gable or ridge vents to let hot air escape;

• One or more windows, though they reduce storage space for wall-hung items;

• Shutters and window boxes, which give the shed a charming cottage look;

• A cupola with weather vane for a bit of country elegance, especially on larger buildings;

• Doors and windows that lock, or maybe even locking shutters.

CONSTRUCTIVE ADVICE

Before you build even a tiny building, bring a set of plans to your local building department and find out if you'll need a building permit. If you hire a contractor, he can take care of this step for you. In some towns, a building permit is required only for buildings larger than 10×12 feet in size, but regulations vary.

Local building codes also dictate the type of foundation needed. Again, requirements differ from town to town, but in most areas buildings

that are 10x10 feet or smaller can be built on concrete block set on the ground. Larger buildings might have to be supported by poured-concrete footings or piers dug down to the frost line. In most towns, the building inspector must examine the trenches or pier holes before you pour the concrete. And if your building plans are involved enough to require wiring or plumbing, the project will be treated much like the construction of a full-size house.

Siting the building is another important consideration too many homeowners overlook. To get the most use out of it, the building may have to be close to the driveway or house; that way, kids are much more likely to put away their bikes and sports equipment, and you won't have to lug tools too far. Never build a shed at the bottom of a hill where the soil gets saturated. And try not to crowd the building by vegetation. Always leave at least 3 feet of open space around all sides—not only will that enable air to circulate freely, reducing mildew, but it will also give you enough clearance to work

ABOVE: This 6×8- foot coop is big enough to house six hens. It was built by youngsters—with plenty of parental help—and includes cozy nesting boxes (RIGHT) that make egg collection easy.

OPPOSITE: Inspired by illustrations in Scandanavian fairy tale books, this 12×12-foot cabin serves as a screenwriter's home office. The columns were cut from dead ash trees nearby.

when it comes time to paint or make repairs. If your building will be close to the house, pay attention to water runoff. Water cascading off the main roof will easily sneak under the roof shingles of your little building. Likewise, place the smaller building so that it won't dump rainfall right at the base of its larger neighbor.

The style of building you choose isn't just a matter of looks, either—there are practical concerns as well. For example, sheds often have relatively

RIGHT: High windows on this outdoor shower bathe the interior in light yet provide plenty of privacy.
BELOW: The roof shingles have a graduated exposure, narrowing to 3 inches at the peak.

ABOVE: **This 10×14-foot garden shed features a post-and-beam frame and T&G pine board siding.**
LEFT: **Half-lap joints at all corners add strength to the frame and the foundation.**

short walls. Those with gable roofs offer taller walls that are useful for putting up shelves and hanging long-handled tools. But they provide little headroom when you stand near the side walls. Gambrel-style roofs, or barn roofs, have shorter walls but much more headroom. If you like the look of a gambrel roof but need plenty of wall storage, get the best of both worlds by ordering the shed with 7- or 8-foot-tall side walls, instead of the shorter walls that are often standard.

One final tip if you're planning a structure that's 10×20 feet or larger: Place the doors in the middle of a sidewall. Doors located in the gable-end wall will make it hard to reach items stored at the very back of the building. ∎

Screened Porches

Build one from scratch, or give your existing porch a new role to play

Hilary and Steve Chasin weren't looking for the usual real estate selling points as they house-hunted in tree-lined Munsey Park, on New York's Long Island. They didn't need a half-dozen bedrooms or a gourmet kitchen. "Basically, we wanted a screened porch with a house attached," says Hilary. And, of course, a protected porch would give this sociable couple a place where they could entertain friends in their beautiful backyard without having to fend off winged invaders.

After looking at every brick Colonial in the neighborhood, they fell in love with a gray, 1935 Georgian-style home—even though it lacked a screened porch. "Fortunately, that was something we could add," says Steve. After buying the house, the couple hired architect T.J. Costello to design a screened-in addition that would connect to a revamped patio in the backyard.

Costello came highly recommended, and had the advantage of living close by—just behind the Chasins' house, in fact. "He would see his work when he looked out his kitchen window," Hilary says with a laugh, "so we knew he'd have a vested interest in making it look good." The project appealed to Costello for another reason as well. "Most people are taking porches and enclosing them," he says. "This is a rare case of creating an old-fashioned screened porch. It's a luxury of the past."

Costello designed the addition to mirror the proportions of an existing kitchen bump-out, which juts from the rear wall on the other side of the patio. The porch roof is supported by four steel-reinforced brick columns at the corners. The brick pattern and grout width match the house and are painted the same shade of gray. "We wanted it to feel like part of the house that was screened in as opposed to something new," says Costello.

The defining elements of the porch are its floor-to-ceiling screens. Framed in cedar, they feature arched muntins designed by Costello. "Besides being fun, they give the porch a form, even if it has transparent walls," he says. The screens offer uninterrupted views of the backyard. "We really wanted a fully screened

OPPOSITE: This screened porch opens into the house through a pair of French doors to brings the outdoors in on sunny days.

ABOVE RIGHT: The exposed beadboard ceiling "makes the space a little more playful," says contractor Tom Murphy.

RIGHT: The porch columns are structural-steel posts surrounded by brick. This beefy structure supports a slate roof.

JOHN BLAIS (3)

room," says Hilary. "When you're in there, the grass is right next to you and the flowers are within smelling distance." Because the screens fit into removable frames, they can be taken down to protect them from winter weather.

Inside, the design is equal parts charm and convenience. The roof sheathing is tongue-and-groove beadboard instead of plywood. The wood is visible between the rafters of the cathedral ceiling. To

On this Victorian porch, screened panels fit gracefully behind the original columns and railings. At summer's end, they're easily removed.

lend practicality to the porch, it includes cable, phone, and electrical outlets "so I can take a work-at-home day and sit out there with my laptop," says Hilary. A ceiling fan equipped with a light keeps things cool in the summer. "Steve doesn't like it hot," she says. "We joked that he'd be waving out at me from the air-conditioned den. I thought the fan might make the porch more palatable to him on steamy days."

REMOVABLE SCREENS

Not everyone has the opportunity—or the budget—to build a screened porch addition. The owners of the 1997 Queen Anne house at left got the same results by turning their existing porch into a screened porch. Large but unobtrusive screened panels were hung behind the porch columns. "This is a fairly typical example of screen-porch technology from the thirties and forties," says Bill Dahn, an architect in Hackensack, New Jersey. "It provides a semipermanent porch enclosure that can be easily removed in the fall and reinstalled in the spring." The appeal of the system lies in its simplicity, says *This Old House* general contractor Tom Silva. "Anyone can install this kind of screen structure—maybe that's why it's coming back into use," says Tom.

The screen frames are made from ⁵⁄₄×3 redwood, with one horizontal brace hidden behind the porch railing. The corners are held together with flat metal angle plates; the screening was stapled to the frame and secured with ¾-inch-wide molding. For even stronger frames, suggests Tom, build them using mortise-and-tenon joints at the corners, or miter the corners and reinforce them with a biscuit joint.

It's important to prime and paint the frames before fitting the screen and molding, however. "This provides full protection for the wood without having to painstakingly paint around the screen," says Tom.

ABOVE LEFT: The panels hang from hooks screwed to the porch beam, and rest behind a quarter-round molding nailed to the floor.
LEFT: A screened porch is a terrific place to entertain in the summer.

Design Ideas For Decks

Consider how you like to live outdoors, then think of a deck as a way to connect your house to the landscape

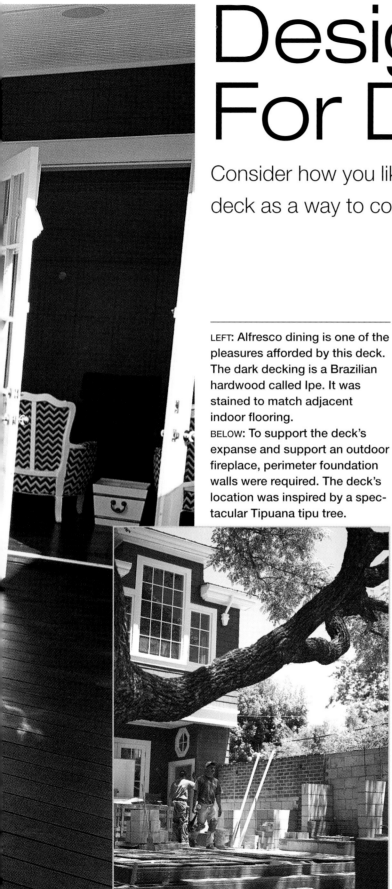

LEFT: Alfresco dining is one of the pleasures afforded by this deck. The dark decking is a Brazilian hardwood called Ipe. It was stained to match adjacent indoor flooring.

BELOW: To support the deck's expanse and support an outdoor fireplace, perimeter foundation walls were required. The deck's location was inspired by a spectacular Tipuana tipu tree.

DAVID ALBANESE (2)

A DECK IS THE QUINTESSENTIAL OUTDOOR ROOM. IT IS a place to stretch out and read or listen to music, relax in a hot tub, eat with family and friends, or simply enjoy the surrounding landscape. Decks can even make a house feel grander and more permanent, as if it has been there longer. Without a deck (or its cousin, the patio), a house can seem more like a bus stop than a destination all its own.

But designing a deck that fulfills so many uses demands a great deal of attention. In fact, some designers say that one of the most challenging aspects of house design is making sure that the transition between indoors and outdoors is handled thoughtfully. Unfortunately, decks (and patios) often end up in no-man's land, that often ignored area where architect and landscape architect each cede responsibility to the other. Homeowners rarely call upon both experts to help with these areas. Instead, they often just order up a raised deck and have a contractor tack it on the back of the house. That approach doesn't respond to the architecture of the house, let alone the surrounding landscape. Instead, it creates deep, weird shadows beneath the decking and ends up looking more like scaffolding.

The grading and the landscaping around a deck or patio are as important as the structure itself. For example, if the house is tucked into the woods, with a low terrace or deck meeting the forest, bring ferns and plantings up to the deck area, and stitch the two together with stepping-stones that lead into the greenery. Or try turning the path into a boardwalk. Or suppose the deck overlooks a large, open area and must provide a transition to a meadow or smooth lawn. All too often, this is when expensive shrubbery is hauled in. A more effective—and usually cheaper—solution is to grade the site cleverly and allow for interesting changes in contour and elevation.

No matter what the site, the key to a good inside-to-outside design is to consider the house, the deck, and the land as parts of a whole, each leading to the next. One way to do this is to continue the character of your home outdoors by using similar materials and design details. That approach inspired the deck shown at left; in effect, the living room floor continues outdoors as the deck. But whatever material you use, be sure it can stand

ABOVE: Built-in planters soften the border between landscape and hardscape.

RIGHT: Using a series of wide stairs and terraces, this hillside deck steps down to a screened pavilion located deep in the woods.

up to sun, moisture, and extreme temperatures. And if it can do that without much maintenance, so much the better.

PERMITS AND CODES

A deck, whether freestanding or attached to the house, is considered a structure and, as such, it must conform to local building codes that could restrict its configuration and size. In many areas of the country, you may need an additional building permit if you plan to add such features as a hot tub, built-in grill, lighting, or refrigerator because of the plumbing and wiring involved. But probably more mistakes are made with deck railings than with any other element of the deck, at least as far as building codes go.

Deck railings are the perfect chance to break away from the ordinary and display your artistic side. Carefully planned, railings can frame a good view or block a bad one, and they can recede into the background or act as outdoor walls. They can be elaborate examples of a carpenter's creativity or take a fashionably minimalist approach. Simply put, they provide a terrific opportunity for you to personalize your home, whatever your vision.

While they are an important visual ingredient in a deck, railings, of course, are first and foremost

JOSHUA McHUGH (3)

a safety feature. The details of their design and construction are spelled out in local building codes.

Generally speaking, elevated decks—typically over 30 inches off the ground—require railings that will keep adults of average stature from taking a header over the edge. Some jurisdictions require railings as high as 42 inches, but most call for a height of 36 inches. Openings between upright or horizontal elements are sized to prevent children from easily crawling through the rails and getting stuck between them. For vertical members, the clearance is from 4 to 6 inches, depending on the jurisdiction. A spacing of 3½ inches or less will eliminate the chance of children getting their head stuck between pickets.

For horizontal components, the typical spacing range is 6 to 9 inches. Railings should also be able to withstand horizontal forces of at least 20 lbs. per square foot. The factors involved: the thickness of the railing material, the distance it spans between rails or posts and how well it is attached. One of the most frequently used ways to attach rails to posts is toenailing, though it's also one of the weakest methods. Better methods include metal connectors; a rail that's mortised into the post and pinned with a nail or screw; or attaching rails to the outside or inside faces of the posts.

HILLSIDE DECK

Chris and Margot Crisman live in a very hilly and wooded area (photo, left). Like most folks with a steeply sloping backyard, they wanted a deck that would make their property more usable. But the Crismans had no desire to tame the rugged terrain with agressive excavation work. Instead, their goal was to reflect and enhance the natural

ABOVE: The destination: a screened pavilion sits at the end of the boardwalk pathway.

ABOVE: Locating the steps within the perimeter of the deck complicated the substructure somewhat, but kept the steps from looking tacked-on.

surroundings, not mask it. "We love our trees and mountainlike property," Chris says, "so we wanted a deck that would help us enjoy nature's beauty." The deck—the long, rambling structure shown on the previous pages—now enables them to walk through the woods as well as sit outside and enjoy it.

The Crismans designed the multilevel structure, then hired a contractor to build it. It features three main elements: a large L-shaped upper level that's attached to the rear of the house, a 12×19-foot midlevel deck, and a 16×16-foot screened pavilion built deep into the woods. The various elements are connected by a series of staircases and boardwalks that deftly wind their way around large boulders and through the thick stand of trees.

The structural elements of the system are pressure-treated southern yellow pine, including 6×6 posts, 2×10 joists and ⁵⁄₄×6-inch decking. All visible surfaces are stained a red-cedar tone. The railing features a 2×6 handrail and 2×2 balusters set in a sunburst pattern. A Victorian-style lamppost helps to guide nighttime wanderers back up to the main house from the screened pavilion.

MAHOGANY DECK

The handsome two-story deck shown at right was designed and built by the father-and-son team of Charles and Jonathan Tabone for the family's

waterfront home in New York state. They wanted a private outdoor spot where they could relax and watch boats sail by. What they didn't want, however, was a typical backyard deck, so they infused the design with traditional front-porch architecture.

For example, the deck has 6-inch square railing posts, a lattice skirt, and tall, round columns, all reminiscent of features found more often at the front of a house. Each of these components was painted white to provide a contrast with the rich, russet color of the red-cedar handrails and mahogany decking.

The 16×18 foot lower-level deck is relatively modest in size, but it offers plenty of living space because of thoughtful proportions. The small niche created by inset stairs, for example, provides an intimate space sized just right for a single lounge chair and a glass of ice tea.

The main deck is located just outside the kitchen, and simplifies the logistics of serving outdoor meals. There's also a short staircase leading up to the deck from an adjoining brick walkway that leads down to the water. The Tabones decided to keep the six-step staircase within the confines of the deck's perimeter framing so it would feel like an intergral part of the deck.

The 14-foot-long upper level balcony deck, built off the upstairs master bedroom suite, is supported by a pair of 12-inch-diameter columns made of structural fiberglass.

LEFT: The project offers a double-decker view of the water.
BELOW: Shade provided by the upper deck offers welcome relief on hot, sunny days.

JOSHUA McHUGH (3)

SEASIDE DECK

In drafting his design for the redwood railing around a deck (right) overlooking the Pacific, designer-builder Scott Padgett had to take into account a local building code mandating a maximum of 4 inches of spacing between every rail. To meet code with the least obstruction to the ocean view, he composed the railing using 2×2s, 2×4s, and 2×6s, painted white for luster and shine. A major design motif is a stepped pattern formed by laying horizontal boards of two different widths across a series of vertical 2×2s erected on either side of the supporting posts (photo, right). The pattern echoes stepped-back elements found elsewhere on the deck, such as a small corner table hung from the deck railing.

The deck's structural scheme, however, was straightforward. Vertical 4×4 posts support continuous top and bottom rails made of 2×4s set on edge, and a cap rail of 2×6s. The pieces immediately above and below the center rail are 2×2s; the center piece is made of 2×4s. All are connected with 3-inch stainless-steel screws. Stainless-steel costs more than galvanized steel, but the fasteners are much more durable, particularly when exposed to the corrosive effects of salt air. Where the railing turns a corner, the railing and rails are free mitered—ther's no extra support behind or beneath the mitered joints.

CLASSIC DECK

The handsome home shown on the following pages sits on a lovely tree-lined street in the historic district of Concord, North Carolina, and was built around 1900. The prize-winning deck built off the rear of the house is a modern addition built by contractor Alex Porter. Yet everything about the deck—its size, railings, and architectural details—would lead you to believe that it was built by an early 20th-century carpenter. And that's exactly what Porter had in mind. "My goal," he says, "was to design and build a deck that looked as if it was original to the house, not recently added on."

The 14-foot-deep structure runs along the rear of the house for about 24 feet, then joins up with a 16×16-foot covered porch. Many of the elements found in the deck and porch were borrowed from the house itself. "The idea to set tapering wooden columns on red-brick piers," explains Porter, "was copied from a porch on the front of the house." The inspiration to cover the knee walls on the new porch with cedar shingles came from the shingled second story. Other architectural details, such as the raised-bevel paneling and border strips around

Custom rails on this seaside deck frame panoramic views of the Pacific Ocean.

the perimeter of the deck, take their cues from features found on millwork inside the house.

The most striking feature of the deck, though, is the series of gracefully shaped balusters that support the deck railing. Porter based the baluster design on the legs of a desk that was built around the same time as the house. He carefully cut out

ABOVE: At the corners of the railing, mitered pieces of 2×6 redwood create an inverted pyramid table that also conceals low-voltage lighting mounted underneath.

DAVID ALBANESE (3)

the redwood balusters with a saber saw, then painstakingly sanded and painted each one before installing it.

REFINING A DECK DESIGN

As you can see from the decks on these pages, there's a lot more to consider on such a project

RIGHT: A prefabricted acrylic hot tub rests 1½ inches below the surface of the deck, and appears to float.

than just where the posts go and what type of decking boards you'll use. The best time to consider special features is long before construction begins. If you wait until after, your wish list will get costly in a hurry. Start the planning process with graph paper and a pencil. Working in scale is useful as you decide exactly where everything should go. Here are some of the amenities you might want to consider:

Built-in benches provide comfortable seating around the perimeter of the deck, especially when accented with cushions and pillows. If it is high enough, the back of the bench may even substitute for a railing, but you'll have to let local codes tell you for sure. Benches may also be placed on either side of a built-in or freestanding table in an area reserved for dining. If you want to integrate storage into the design, construct benches with lids instead of fixed seats.

Built-in planters are a handsome element often used to punctuate or terminate a long bench run; they can also accent sets of steps or corners where two sections of railing meet. Fill them with colorful annuals, with herbs useful in outdoor cooking, or with evergreen shrubs or small trees to help create a year-round privacy shield. Finally, consider installing lighting under railings or alongside steps as a safety measure; a balanced mix of light fixtures will also enhance the look and mood of the deck after dark. The installation of low-voltage wiring may not require a permit, but anything else most likely will.

Outdoor speakers have only recently become commonplace. Sure, you could drag out a boom box and extension cord and assault everyone's ears with tinny, low-fidelity sound. Or, you could fill the air with high-quality audio using pairs of permanently mounted outdoor speakers connected to an indoor stereo.

LEFT: Details, like the raised-bevel paneling and border strips that accent the stairs, were borrowed from millwork inside the house.

Weather-resistant outdoor speakers have been available for decades, but recent improvements in long-term durability and sound quality have caused them to be much more popular than ever. The number of options has also expanded. In addition to the traditional off-white or box-shaped speakers, manufacturers have come out with "stealth" versions. Some are shaped like faux rocks

LEFT: **Outdoor lighting can emphasize a deck's features while improving its safety.**

ABOVE RIGHT: **The shaped balusters are based on the design of legs on an antique desk.**

that blend into backyard landscapes, others are hidden in hanging plants or shelf planters.

Although indoor and outdoor speakers both do essentially the same thing, indoor speakers are designed for use in a confined space, while outdoor speakers have to disperse sound over a much wider area—and do it after being drenched, baked, and blasted by Mother Nature.

Large speaker cabinets help music to sound more natural, but at the same time, speakers shouldn't be visually obtrusive. For the 15-by-25-foot deck at a *This Old House* project in Billerica, Massachusets, for instance, two speakers about 8 inches square and 11 inches tall do the job.

On long runs to remote locations, bury speaker wires 6 to 12 inches deep (or deeper if code requires) so they won't be a tripping hazard. Only Mylar-sheathed, "direct-burial" wire will do in these circumstances—PVC-covered over-the-counter wires won't last. At the Billerica project, a 4-inch PVC pipe was buried between the house and the as-yet-speakerless pool area. If speakers are added later on, it will be an easy matter to fish wires through the pipe.

Outdoor heating helps to stretch a deck's usefulness into the chillier seasons as well as make it more comortable when cool night air encroaches. The solution is a patio heater, a device originally marketed to restaurateurs who wanted to extend their outdoor dining season. Some radiate heat up to 12 feet away and can elevate the temperature of the surrounding area 15° to 20°F. The heaters, some of which stand almost eight feet high, are fueled by propane gas that can either be supplied either from an in-ground or aboveground tank or from a smaller cylinder attached to the unit, allowing it to be easily moved from place to place. Each cylinder will fuel from six to ten hours of use. The heat comes from an infrared radiant-heating element, and safety features include a push-button ignition and a switch that automatically shuts the unit off if the pilot light goes out.

For a wood-burning heating alternative, consider a chiminea. Originally used in Mexico as bread ovens, these portable wood-burning outdoor fireplaces can bring just the right touch of light and warmth to your new deck. ▪

Materials For Decks

There are still plenty of choices, but the most common one will soon be gone

REDWOOD has natural insect and decay resistance, old-growth more so than second-growth. It is the most expensive outdoor wood in most parts of the country.

WESTERN HEMLOCK, a treated species often used in western states, does not accept preservatives easily, so cuts are made in it to enable the chemical to penetrate.

CEDAR is widely available, and one of the premier untreated woods.

F
OR MOST HOMEOWNERS, BUYING LUMBER FOR A DECK project is a mysterious process—the multitude of choices can bewilder even professionals. "Knowing what to buy," admits *This Old House* contractor Tom Silva, "requires some knowledge, patience, and common sense, whether you're looking for studs to frame a partition or joists and decking for a porch."

Choosing good lumber inevitably involves the art of compromise. Over the years, Tom has seen a general decline in the quality of available lumber. "You have to have a good eye or you can easily get taken," he says. "When I scan a piece, I look closely for loose knots, big knots, checks, and cracks. I want lumber that is good and straight and has as few knots as possible, especially near the edges." Tom's purchasing begins with what he calls "shopping the ends." At the lumberyard, he carefully eyeballs the painted ends on a stack lumber. "Knots in the ends are going to give me problems when it comes to cutting and nailing," he says. He also looks for

BELOW LEFT: This boardwalk combines treated wood and plastic lumber. The pilings and rail supports are made of fiberglass-reinforced plastic, while the load-bearing stringers and the railings are pressure-treated southern yellow pine. The decking and top rail are composite lumber.

DARRIN HADDAD (2)

SOUTHERN YELLOW PINE infused with various preservatives is the least expensive treated wood and by far the most widely used.

PLASTIC Plastic lumber often consists of unpigmented plastic recycled from milk containers.

COMPOSITE LUMBER is a blend of sawdust and recycled plastic from various sources; it accepts paint or stain.

splits and deep cracks that can weaken the wood.

Pulling a 2×6 from an opened stack, he lays his hand palm-down across the width of the board. "I can immediately tell by feel whether a board is cupped," he says. "If it isn't flat from edge to edge, I don't want it." Warping along the length of a board can be troublesome as well. When Tom sights down the edge of the 2×6, he discovers the wood is slightly arched from end to end, or crowned. That's bad news for a decking board but not always so bad for a joist. With the apex of the crown arched upward, the joist would eventually straighten out and help prevent sag in the deck. "Just make sure you install the crown up," says Tom. "Long ago, my brothers and I had finished building a deck with my dad, when he noticed a dip in the floor system. Sure enough, we had put in one joist with its crown going the wrong way and it sagged like a swayback horse. He made us rip it out and turn it over. After that, I never forget to check crown."

Tom says that, above all, lumber shoppers should avoid buying wet wood. "If I pick up a board and it it feels unusually heavy, I know it's soaked. That means it's going to shrink or warp when it dries out." For new construction, Tom frames with stock graded to have no more than a 19 percent moisture content.

The way a board was milled is another factor Tom takes into consideration. Most lumber comes from logs that have been flat sawn, producing boards with end grain nearly parallel with the face. The milling process is fast and yields a wide range of products—posts, framing lumber, boards—with little waste. Compared with quartersawn lumber, however, flat-sawn pieces are more likely to warp as a board dries or to blister paint with changes in humidity.

Dividing a log lengthwise into quarters is a slow and expensive milling process that produces lumber prized for its stability and beautiful grain. On each board, the tree rings run at nearly right angles to the face, so the wood is less likely to cup or twist. This premium-priced lumber is in short supply at most lumberyards but can be purchased by special order. "Anytime I want a board that won't expand and contract too much—on decking, flooring, trim—I look for that vertical grain," says Tom. "The wood also looks great if you use a stain to show off the grain."

CHOOSING A WOOD SPECIES

A typical house is a symphony of woods brought together to perform according to their particular strengths. No single tree species yields lumber with all these varied characteristics at an affordable price, so Tom picks different woods based on their intended use. For deck and porch framing, where resisting rot is paramount, he buys pressure-treated southern yellow pine. Clear, vertical-grain Douglas fir is Tom's favorite choice for porch decking that will be protected from the weather. For exposed decking, he uses redwood, cedar, or pressure-treated yellow pine. Another deck wood Tom likes is plantation-grown Ipe, a tropical hardwood so dense that nails need drilled pilot holes.

THE NEW PRESSURE-TREATED

Among building materials, wood is ideal: beautiful, strong, easily shaped. And it's renewable. Its one big flaw is vulnerability to decay and insects. In the 1930s, scientists found a way to infuse wood with a solution that included copper (toxic to the fungi that cause rot) and arsenic (then the most common insecticide). They also added chromium, which triggered a chemical reaction that locked the pesticides into the wood.

The formula became known as chromated copper arsenate, or just CCA. The industry called it pressure-treated because the chemicals were forced into the wood under great pressure. The wood dried with a green tint because of the copper, but otherwise it was similar to ordinary lumber—except that it stood up to even the dampest, warmest climates. For decades, pressure-treated wood remained a specialty product, but as the price of cedar and redwood soared, sales of the greenish lumber ballooned.

In the late 1980s, however, researchers discovered that acids, even the acid rain common in the Northeast, could reverse the chemical reactions binding chemicals to the wood, thus allowing some of the arsenic to leach out into the soil. Early in 2002, the Environmental Protection Agency announced that it was requiring a phaseout of CCA. The treated-wood industry will have until December 2003 to stop selling CCA-treated lumber for residential use.

What will replace CCA? The new generation of chemical mixes includes several without arsenic or chromium, including ammoniacal copper quartenary (ACQ). Some, such as ACQ, are "pretty much one-to-one substitutes" for chromated copper arsenate, says Jerrold Winandy, of the Forest Products Laboratory. You can expect these products to be increasingly available.

Meanwhile, homeowners concerned about potential arsenic problems aren't being encouraged by the EPA to rip out existing CCA-treated woodwork. Instead, the EPA suggests that homeowners

How to read lumber

All these 2×10s were graded as No. 2 lumber and should be strong enough for joists despite various defects, easier to see in this untreated sampling. Joists under a deck, however, should ideally be pressure-treated southern yellow pine.

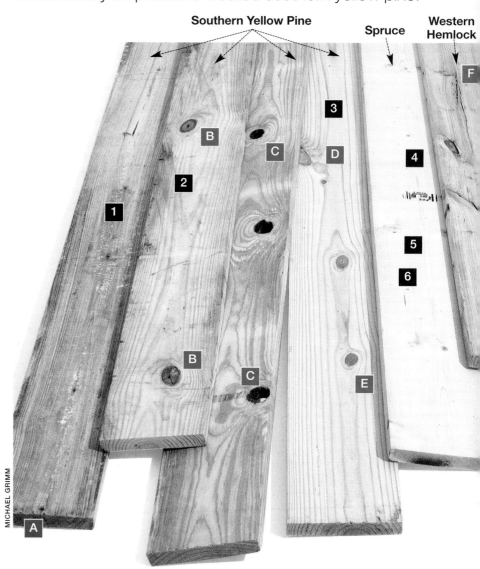

MICHAEL GRIMM

STRUCTURAL DEFECTS

A. SPLIT: A cross-grain break all the way through a piece.

B. ENCASED KNOT: Growth rings are separate from surroounding wood.

C. KNOTHOLE: A void left by a dead branch.

D. REACTION WOOD: Grain that turns toward the edge.

E. INTERGROWN KNOT: Shares growth ring with surrounding wood.

F. SHAKE: A separation between growth rings.

G. SPIKE KNOT: An embedded branch, sawn lengthwise.

COSMETIC DEFECTS

1. PITCH: Resin that has oozed to the surface.

2. BLUE STAIN: Discoloration caused by fungus.

3. CHECKING: Surface cracks commonly caused by drying stresses.

4. PIN KNOT: A knot less than ½ inch in diameter.

5. TORN GRAIN: Roughened surface where a planer or saw pulled wood out of the board instead of slicing it smooth.

6. BARK POCKET: Encapsulated tree skin; not a problem if small.

may want to coat exposed surfaces on a regular basis. According to the agency, some studies suggest that regular applications of penetrating coatings (such as oil-based, semitransparent stains), may reduce migration of preservative chemicals.

As for future projects, buy the wood that is best suited to a given situation. Off the ground,

To check a board for warping and crown, Tom Silva sights down one edge.

ordinary pine works fine for vertical elements like deck balusters, especially if it's brushed with a water repellent and then painted or stained. For decks themselves, cedar and redwood look better than pressure-treated wood but cost more. Where lives depend on rot-free supports—such as posts and framing under decks—pressure-treated wood still makes sense. Just be sure to take any precautions recommended by the manufacturer when you cut or handle it. One tip is to cut over a plastic tarp so it can be rolled up along with the sawdust and thrown in the trash.

A NEW WORLD OF DECKING

Substitutes for wood decking have been around for at least 10 years, and the number of products increases every year. That's partly due to the fact that nonwood decking is easy to maintain, very weather resistant, and won't warp or splinter. These products aren't inexpensive, however, at least compared with the current cost of pressure-treated lumber. Also, consider the fact that the spacing of deck joists and other framing members will depend on the nonwood decking you choose; each has its own span requirements. The same goes for installation techniques, so make sure you read the literature correctly.

But the biggest problem you might encounter with these materials is finding a broad choice in your area—not all are widely available. To help you make sense of what's on the market, we've arranged these products into three categories. Products within the same category might not look alike, but they tend to share similar working and performance characteristics.

Composite decking Composites are the most widely used alternative to real wood. They are a blend of wood fiber and plastic that's extruded to form boards, balusters, and even handrails. They're weather resistant, and cleaning involves little more than some light scrubbing or a quick blast from a pressure washer. Perhaps the best testament to the durability of composite decking is that it has been successfully used in national parks and on seaside boardwalks for years.

Of all the alternative decking materials, composite boards are most like real wood in their appearance as well as in how they're installed. Though somewhat denser than wood, they can still be cut with carbide-tipped blades and bits, and they're attached to joists with screws, nails, or any of the hidden deck-fastening systems used for wood. Because they're made of wood fiber, composite boards will change color to a silvery gray two to three months after installation. Some of the products accept stain that will mask this.

Many composite boards give the impression of wood from a distance, but up close they tend towards blandness. Some count this uniform appearance as an advantage, however, likening it to the uniform appearance of straight-grained natural woods such as redwood.

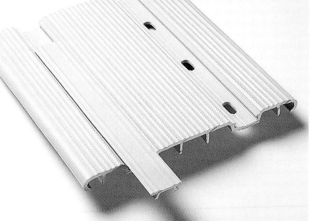

ABOVE: **Composite boards from (1) TimberTech, (2) Nexwood, (3) Trex, (4) Choicedek.**
LEFT: Vinyl-decking planks simply snap into place.

Plastic and vinyl decking Technically speaking, plastic decking is made of either HDPE or PVC (polyvinyl chloride—the same material used to make plastic drainpipes). These products have thin walls and hollow profiles, so they are lighter than composites. Plastic decks require even less maintenance than composites—manufacturers recommend spring cleaning with a sponge mop. Some of the products are backed by warranties that run as long as 50 years.

Most of the products look nothing like real wood, but many people find their lighter colors more appealing than the classic wood tones. One pro who installed such a deck at his own home chose the light-colored planking because it

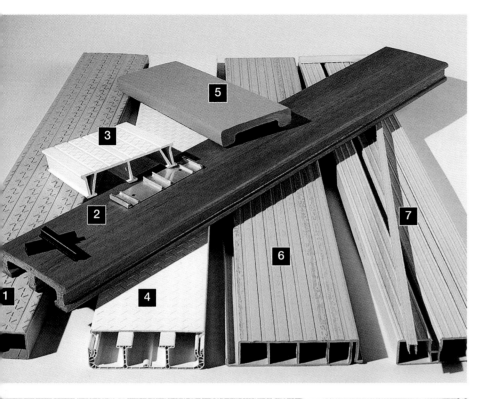

LEFT: Plastic decking from (1) DreamDeck, (2) Extrudawood, (3) Brock Deck, (4) Homescape, (5) Carefree, (6) Westtech, (7) DreamDeck.
BELOW LEFT: E-Z Deck resembles plastic decking, but is made of fiberglass and polyester resin.

matched his vinyl siding. "Unlike the wood decks I've installed previously, this plastic deck hasn't gone gray," he added.

But working with plastic decking is very different. For starters, to cut vinyl boards and end up with a smooth edge, you need a carbide-tooth blade with 18 to 24 teeth. And because boards have a high rate of expansion and contraction, manufacturers recommend a ¼-inch gap between boards and at the end of every 8-foot run.

Since planks are hollow, they typically can't be ripped at a taper to fit an out-of-square wall or inside corner (although some can be ripped to a uniform width along a structural rib). Laying out and installing the planks can be tricky because with some systems you must end on a whole plank. Finishing or trimming end cuts can also be a problem—look for systems that have end caps to conceal hollow ends and movement-related gaps. As with composite wood, the joist-spacing requirements vary. Some products require support every 12 inches, while others can span 32 inches, so make sure you pick the decking system before framing the deck. And nearly every manufacturer uses a different type of proprietary fastening system. In most systems, the fasteners are hidden once the deck is completed.

Fiberglass fecking Unlike the other alternatives, fiberglass decking is actually stronger than wood. Made of fiberglass and polyester resin, the planks will easily span 24 inches. Chris Myers, a decking contractor based in Los Angeles, switched over to the product because of the polished look he can create with it. "With 40-foot-long planks," he says, "I can make a clean, seamless deck." Unlike plastic decking, he adds, fiberglass boards are less affected by thermal expansion.

Not surprisingly, fiberglass requires a special fastening system: fiberglass strips attached to the tops of the joists with 1½-inch galvanized screws. The decking snaps in place over the strips. "The system takes a little getting used to," says Myers, "but it makes for a fast installation."

For now, alternative decking seems to be an option worth considering if you really hate cleaning and maintaining a wood deck, or if you live in an area that's particularly hostile to wood. Meanwhile, the use of these decking materials seems to be a trend that's here to stay.

Deck Construction Basics

Here's how to build a time-saving deck with a floating foundation, and how to plan an attached deck on piers

W HAT COULD BE MORE EMBLEMATIC OF OUTDOOR living than a backyard deck? For many land-scaping plans, a deck is the key that unlocks the utility of an underutilized yard. Though not as durable as a masonry patio, a wood deck makes up for this in sheer versatility. Where a patio is typically built at grade level, a deck is able to cascade down a hill-side, spread out in terraces over a flat yard, or even extend from a second-story bedroom to capture a view. In fact, there are few sites on which a deck can't be built.

The very range of design possibilties and construction vari-ables, however, can be intimidating. Sometimes a deck must be attached to the house…and sometimes not. The size of sup-ports—posts, beams, and joists—varies considerably in size and spacing. The deck boards, once limited to a few types of durable woods, are now available in splendid variety, including plantation-grown tropical hardwoods and various nonwood alternatives (see page 156). And you may not want to just nail the boards down—there are at least four alternatives that keep fasteners from ever showing. For example, one involves the use of stainless-steel spikes that lock the edge of each board to a joist. So consider the following guide as your primer to deck building construction. Once you understand the basics, consult with your building department and work out the details.

A GRADE-LEVEL DECK

The simplest type of deck to build is one that sits just above grade. Its structural requirements are modest, and it can sometimes even rest on precast piers that sit on the ground. This timesaving construction method, shown

The standard combination of portland cement, gravel, and sand is an excellent material for setting deck posts. A 60-pound bag yields 1 cubic foot of concrete.

This elevated deck is supported by posts, beams, and joists. Any deck more than 30 inches above grade (measured to the top of the decking) must have railings. In this case, the grade was raised considerably at a later stage of construction.

JAMES WORRELL

at right, is called a floating-foundation system, and the deck is not attached to the house. The system is allowed by building codes nationwide, including regions where frost heaving is a concern, but only in locations where the site is fairly level.

The advantage of the system, of course, is speed: The 12×16-foot deck shown here was built in a weekend. The first day involved setting the precast concrete piers and building the understructure framing. These piers have a channels in the top that hold the joists; standard piers incorporate a nailing block or some other device to secure the joists. Joists are the framing members that support the decking itself. For a quick explanation of deck anatomy, see the drawing on pages 168–169.

The deck is suppported by six rows of piers laid parallel with the house. The rows are 25½ in. apart, and each one consists of five piers. The most accurate way to lay out the 30 piers is to set the four corner piers first.

Start by placing the two corner piers alongside the house foundation, spacing them 14 feet on center so the 16-foot floor joist will overhang 1 foot on each end. That way, the decking will partially conceal the piers and make the structure appear to float above the ground. Temporarily place a perfectly straight joist into the slots in the piers, then check the board for level. If needed, dig out some dirt from under the high pier to level the joist.

You might also have to dig out from under the piers to ensure that the finished decking will be at least 1 inch or so below the threshold of a door. Once the joist is properly positioned, install three intermediate piers. These piers should be equally spaced between the two corner piers.

Next, set the two outside corner piers farthest from the house. Temporarily install a good, straight 2×6 joist between an outside corner pier and one of the piers alongside the house. Then move the outside corner pier left or right as needed until the joist is perfectly square, forming a 90-degree angle with the house.

Check to see if the joist is level. If the outside corner pier is high, dig out a little dirt; if it's low by a couple of inches, cut a 4×4 post to fit between the pier and joist. After you've leveled the joist, install four intermediate piers equally spaced between the corner ones. Repeat this process for the remaining outside corner pier on the other side of the structure. Once you get the hang of it, you'll find that the work goes quickly.

You'll now have three rows of piers installed: one along the house and one coming out from each side of the deck. Lay in all the joists, level them, and install the intermediate piers (photos, above).

ABOVE: **Joists are set into premolded slots in the concrete piers.**
RIGHT: **Trim the decking ends with a circular saw. Boards should overhang the band joist by at least ½ inch.**

Next, screw a band joist across the ends of the floor joists at both the left and right sides of the frame. Move to the joist farthest from the house and screw short outriggers—12-inch-long 2×6 blocks—in place. Install one at each of the five piers, then attach the final band joist at each end of the deck. That detail allows the decking to extend past the piers so they're less conspicuous.

Installing the 2×6 decking is the second phase of construction (it took less than four hours on this project). First, arrange all the deck boards on the joists. If the boards are wet, butt them tightly together; they'll shrink as they dry out, and gaps will form between each board. If the decking is dry, leave a ⅛- to ¼-inch space between the boards.

Shift the decking so the first and last boards overhang the left and right side band joists an equal amount. Also align the ends of all the boards along the house, leaving about 1 inch of space between decking and the siding. Then attach the boards with 3-inch galvanized screws. Finally, snap a line across the outer ends of the boards and trim them straight with a circular saw.

That's all there is to building a deck on a floating foundation. The basic assembly techniques are common to most decks, but if your site slopes, you'll have some additional work to do.

DECK WITH CONCRETE PIERS

A multilevel deck, or an elevated deck on a sloping site, needs more structural support than a floating deck. Part of that support comes from the house itself: One side is firmly attached to the framing. The rest of the support comes from poured concrete piers that support each post and hold it slightly above the grade—this reduces problems associated with rot. The piers are made by pouring concrete into a cylindrical hole. In cold climates, the bottom of the hole should be at a depth just below frost line; otherwise, alternating freeze/thaw cycles will push it out of position.

To minimize the number of piers, elevated decks incorporate a system of intermediate structural members called beams. Posts support the widely-spaced beams, and piers support the posts. Even a fairly large elevated deck won't call for a lot of piers, so it usually isn't worthwhile to have the concrete delivered by a ready-mix truck. Instead, you can mix your own from bags of dry concrete mix and water.

You'll find many varieties of concrete mix at your local home center, but all have one ingredient in common: portland cement—a fine, flourlike powder that gives concrete its color and rock-hard strength. Natural cement— as opposed to the manufactured, portland variety—was discovered by the Romans, who mined it from pumice deposits on the slopes of Mount Vesuvius and elsewhere. Today, instead of relying on volcanoes, manufacturers bake the necessary minerals (calcium, silicon, aluminum and iron) in giant rotating kilns heated to 2800° Fahrenheit. Roman builders found they could stretch their precious supply of cement—and make it stronger—by adding crushed

Check to make sure that the frame is square and each joist is level. Don't be afraid to make minor corrections. Unlike decks with poured concrete footings, this system allows all the parts to be repositioned or adjusted even after the understructure framing is completed. Once you're satisfied with the framing, backfill around any piers that were dug into the ground.

TWO GOOD WAYS TO ATTACH A DECK TO A HOUSE

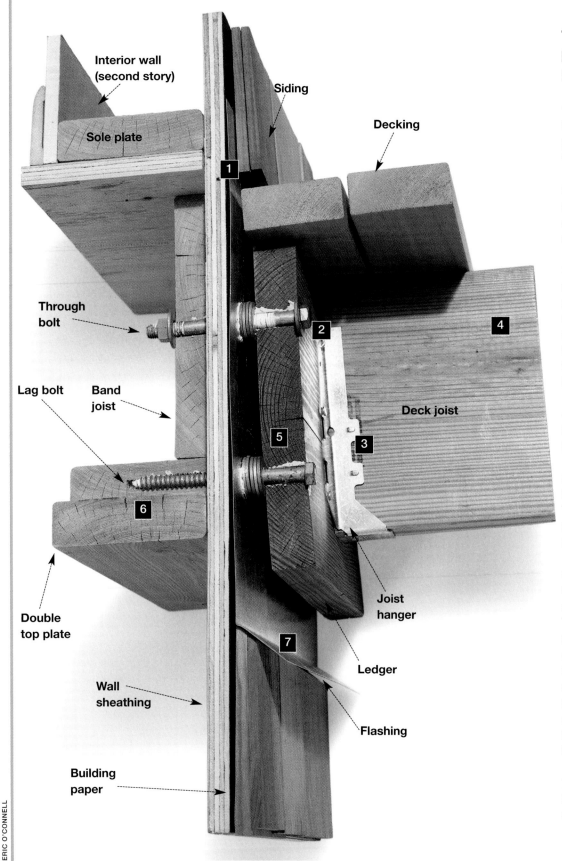

Interior wall (second story)

Siding

Decking

Sole plate

Through bolt

Lag bolt

Band joist

Deck joist

Double top plate

Joist hanger

Ledger

Wall sheathing

Flashing

Building paper

1 2 3 4 5 6 7

1. The system developed by researchers at the USDA Forest Products Laboratory

1. Tuck flashing under exterior siding. Use galvanized flashing, because copper-laden runoff from pressure-treated wood will corrode aluminum over time.

2. Use ½-inch-diameter bolts with nuts and washers wherever possible, for extra strength. Insert two to four washers as spacers so the ledger won't trap water.

3. Attach joist hangers using nails specified by the manufacturer. To avoid penetrating flashing with long nails, either attach the hangers and then hammer over the nail tips before bolting the ledger to the house, or switch to short, thick fasteners, called hanger nails, as directed by the joist hanger manufacturer.

4. Use pressure-treated lumber for beams and joists. The lumber shown here is an arsenic-free type.

5. After installing flashing, temporarily hang the ledger in order to drill bolt holes. Then remove the ledger, squirt caulk in the holes and immediately reposition the ledger in order to tighten the bolts.

6. Where access on both sides of the wall is limited, ½-inch-diameter lag bolts may be used instead of through bolts. They must reach at least 1½ inches into solid lumber—the band joist, top plate, or studs. This photo shows connections for an elevated deck attached to the second-floor band joist. Lower decks may call for lag bolts or through bolts, in combination with expanding anchor bolts where the ledger is attached to a foundation wall.

7. Extend the metal flashing below the ledger and bend the lip out to drain water away from the siding.

2. Tom Silva's System

Adding a deck to a house in Lexington, Massachustts, *This Old House* contractor Tom Silva also pays particular attention to the ledger that connects the deck to the house and carries all the supporting joists. "It's where 99 percent of mistakes are made," he says.

TOP: Because a ledger pressed tight against a house can trap moisture and encourage rot, Tom creates a gap for air with spacers shaped to fit the recessed foundation of the house. He cuts the spacers from scraps of pressure-treated wood, nails them on and then drills two holes through each spacer and the ledger, one hole near the top edge, another at the bottom.

MIDDLE: Tom and his nephew, Charlie Silva, jockey the ledger into position. Aiming through the top holes previously made, they drill into the sill plate of the house and install lag bolts. Through the lower holes, they install masonry anchor bolts into the concrete foundation.

BOTTOM: For flashing, Tom uses an adhesive-backed flexible membrane made of polyethylene film and rubberized asphalt. Tom prefers it to metal flashing because its sticky nature makes a water-tight seal around bolts that penetrate it. Since the material could degrade in sunlight, however, he takes care not to leave it exposed. To prevent rot, Tom constructs the entire deck frame from pressure-treated material; wood treated with CCA preservative is bring phased out, and will be replaced by ACQ, a safer alternative.

stone, gravel, and sand, and today's concrete is not much different. A typical 60-pound bag of the basic mix contains 1 part cement, 2 to 3 parts sand, and 3 to 5 parts gravel or rock, depending on the mix; it yields 1 cubic foot of concrete.

This Old House contractor Tom Silva follows some simple rules when mixing concrete by hand. First, he pours the dry mix into a wheelbarrow and stirs it to blend the gravel that settles in shipping. Then, into a little crater he forms in the mix, Tom adds clean water, which he chops in thoroughly with a hoe or shovel. "You want to add the water slowly, in stages, as you mix," he says. After a few minutes of churning, the wet concrete should be uniformly stiff—like peanut butter—with no dry spots. Tom adds a bit more water if the concrete is crumbly; if it's soupy, he'll put in more dry mix.

Stirring concrete is hard work. "If you aren't breaking a sweat, then you aren't mixing it right," Tom says. To ease the task, many people over-water, but the waterlogged concrete just ends up weaker and more susceptible to shrinking, cracking, and abrasion. Once water is added, a basic dry mix sets in about 90 minutes, depending on the weather. Heat speeds the process; cold slows it down. After pouring the mix in a hole, Tom jabs it half a dozen times with a steel rod to consolitate it, then inserts a post anchor—a metal bracket used to connect the pier to a post.

Properly mixed and cared for, concrete takes 28 days to reach its required compressive strength—at least 2,000 pounds per square inch. After that, hardening will proceed for years, albeit very slowly, as the cement continues to cure.

DECK FRAMING BASICS

The deck shown on page 163 is only partially complete, but eventually offered a commanding view of a pool, a fish pond, and thick woods behind the new house. But what's immediately apparent to a visitor stepping onto the deck is its rich, dark wood—firm as stone and utterly free of knots—and the airy cedar pergola overhead, with its ever-changing play of shadow and light. And beneath this deck's deceptively straightforward design lies Tom Silva's inventive, no-shortcut building methods. "I've torn down too many decks that were falling apart after just seven or ten years," says Tom. "That's not going to happen with this one."

To that end, he uses robust materials and innovative techniques that can withstand decades of wet weather. "Water is the enemy," Tom says, and his defenses against it are as rigorous as those around a medieval castle. For instance, Tom put half-inch blocks behind the ledger—the pressure-treated 2×10 that holds the deck to the house— to keep water from being trapped there. And instead of using traditional metal flashing to protect the plywood sheathing from melting snow and splashing rain, he applied a rubbery sheet of bitumen-impregnated plastic typically used on roofs (see sidebar, page 167).

Tom also made sure the deck slopes slightly away from the family room. "Slanting it by even half a bubble will do the job," he says refering to the marks on the level's vial. "It's supposed to be standard practice, but you'd be surprised at how many new decks are completely level."

THE CRITICAL CONNECTION

The most important element of an elevated deck is the ledger: the deck's connection to the house. If a ledger is installed improperly—and many are—the entire deck can collapse just when the potential for injury is greatest: when a crowd gathers. But a deck can handle the rowdiest gang of fraternity brothers as long as the ledger is properly connected to the side of the house. Robert Falk, a structural engineer with the USDA Forest Products Laboratory in Madison, Wisconsin, looked into the problem of deck failures after hearing of a deck-related death. Using a database to search five years of newspaper articles from around the country, he found that nearly every collapsed deck had been attached with nails, rather than bolts, and that investigators had pinpointed the nails as the cause of collapse. "On paper, you can calculate that nails will work," Falk says. "In practice, it's a different story."

As people gather on a deck, their weight and movement translate not just into a downward force but also into an outward force that acts as a lever prying the deck away from the house. Nails work well to resist the downward force but are no match for the outward force. Held in place only by the friction of bent wood fibers, nails tend to loosen when wood alternately shrinks and swells with changes in moisture content and temperature. In contrast, a lag bolt, which looks like a giant screw, has as much as nine times the pullout resistance of a nail for every inch of penetration, Falk says. Better still is the metal-to-metal connection of a through bolt, inserted in a drilled hole and fitted with a nut and a flat washer on the other side. Placing a washer on both sides spreads the pulling force over an even larger portion of the beam. "You'd rip the whole structure apart before those bolts would pull out," Falk says.

Both of these connectors offer an extra benefit over nails: They don't suddenly pull out as wood

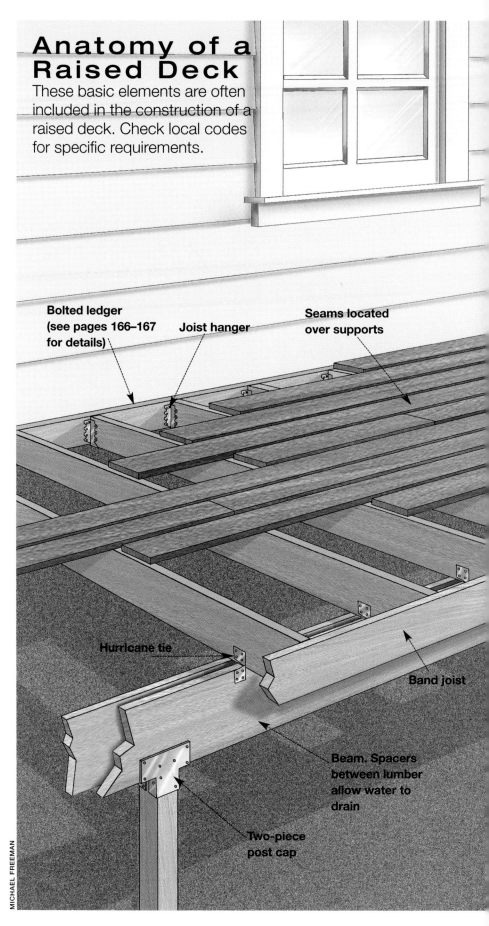

Anatomy of a Raised Deck

These basic elements are often included in the construction of a raised deck. Check local codes for specific requirements.

Bolted ledger (see pages 166–167 for details)

Joist hanger

Seams located over supports

Hurricane tie

Band joist

Beam. Spacers between lumber allow water to drain

Two-piece post cap

MICHAEL FREEMAN

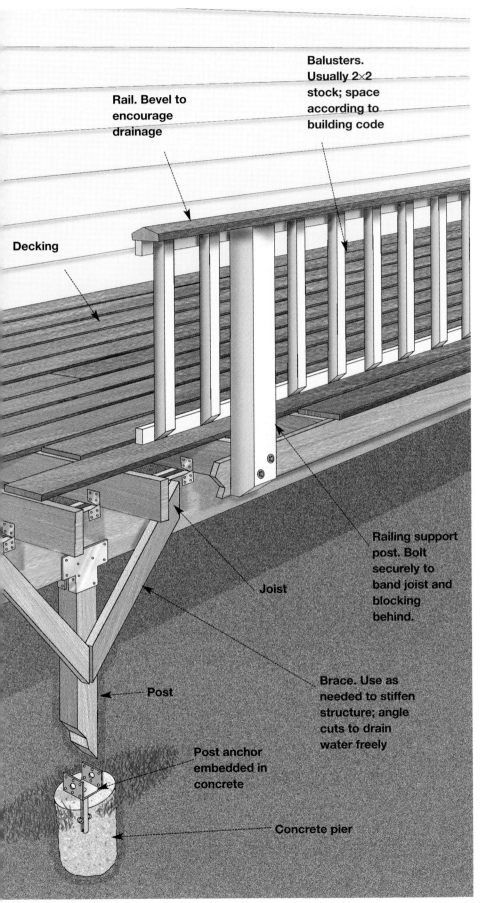

Rail. Bevel to encourage drainage

Balusters. Usually 2×2 stock; space according to building code

Decking

Railing support post. Bolt securely to band joist and blocking behind.

Joist

Brace. Use as needed to stiffen structure; angle cuts to drain water freely

Post

Post anchor embedded in concrete

Concrete pier

shrinks and swells. But they may loosen over time. If the deck is inspected annually, early signs of loosening will show up as a widening gap against the house. To see two methods for attaching the ledger solidly, turn to pages 166–167.

BEAMS, JOISTS, AND DECKING

The drawing at left shows how the various structural elements—post, beams, and joists—work together to support the decking. The exact spacing of each element is based on its span and dimension. The structural portions of a deck are governed more by their strength than by their appearance, so Tom typically uses pressure-treated lumber (for more on recent changes regarding this product, see page 158). Though connections are often made by toenailing (driving a nail through one piece and into another at an angle), Tom uses galvanized metal brackets and ties whenever possible. "They're a lot stronger than nails alone," he says, "and the connection is less likely to loosen up over time."

There are plenty of choices when it comes to choosing and installing the decking (see page 156). For the deck on page 163, Tom laid down deck boards made of ipe ("EE-pay"), a hard, chocolate-colored Brazilian hardwood with a legendary reputation for durability. (It covers the famous boardwalk in Atlantic City.) The 1×4 boards have an estimated 40-year lifespan, nearly twice that of pressure-treated yellow pine, and cost roughly the same as clear redwood. But there's a downside to ipe's incredible density: It's impossible to hammer a nail or drive a screw through it without first drilling a pilot hole.

DECK SKIRTING

The space beneath elevated decks is sometimes enclosed with some lattice screen or spaced wood slats. This enclosure, called the skirt, conceals the framing without obstructing air circulation under the decking.

A skirt typically consists of a wood lattice panel set into a wood frame. Sometimes the lattice is attached directly to cleats nailed to the structural framing, but without a frame, lattice is susceptible to warping and damage because the lattice has very little support.

The easiest way to install framed lattice is to nail the sections to the existing post structure. But a better solution is to mount at least one of the panels on either 3- or 4-inch galvanized strap- or T-hinges screwed to the rim joists. The swing up frames make repairs easy, and they also let you use space below the deck for storage.

Finishes For Wood

Choose the right finish for decks and other outdoor wood, and maintain it

OUTDOOR WOOD IS AT RISK THE MOMENT THE LAST nail is driven home. Moisture swells it, the sun drys it out and shrinks it, and enemies such as ultraviolet light and mildew work relentlessly to change its color. Little wonder that so much time and effort is spent on putting one sort of finish or another on wood. For many years the choices were slim: You could paint it, stain it, or just leave it alone. But now you'll find a host of effective, durable new products for decks, siding, and fences. Unfortunately, the distinctions between various types are often blurry, so here's a guide that will help you understand the various options.

The basic ingredients of every exterior finish are remarkably similar. Most rely on three basic elements: oils—natural linseed or tung oils, or synthetic resins—to resist moisture; preservatives containing zinc, iodine, borates, and other compounds to discourage mildew, moss, and mold; and a combination of ultraviolet-absorbing and -blocking ingredients for the toughest task of all—blocking UV degradation. UV light breaks down lignin, the natural glue that holds wood fibers together, and eventually turns all wood left outdoors as gray as barnboard. In paints and stains, pigments block UV the same way a long-sleeve shirt protects exposed skin from sunburn. Clear finishes behave more like sunscreen: They contain chemicals that absorb UV radiation, at least for a time. "The organic molecules can only handle so many photons before they fall apart," says Mark Knaebe, a chemist with extensive experience in evaluating outdoor finishes at the U.S.D.A Forest Products Laboratory. Once UV-absorbers lose their effectiveness—in as little as a few months in sunny climates—the rays pass through unhindered and start to deteriorate the wood surface. Then it's only a matter of time before the finish itself loses its grip.

Adding pigment is the surest way to block UV over the long run. If it closely matches the natural color of the wood and is used in limited quantity, it isn't noticeable and can be added even to "clear" finishes. Add more, however, and the finish begins to darken the wood grain and resemble a stain.

The working ingredients of a finishing product are suspended in a solvent—either oil or water—so you can brush or spray them on wood. Which solvent you select depends on your priorities, however. "Oil-based finishes," according to Knaebe,

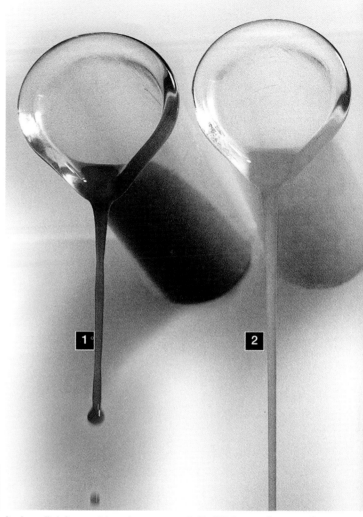

ERIC AXENE

A clear finish must be chosen carefully if it is used on outdoor woodwork: (1) Urethane: Forms a hard film. (2) Penetrating sealer: High solids content improves durability. (3) Hybrid: The first coat soaks in; the second provides a protective film. (4) Varnish: This ancient film-forming product requires multiple coats for beauty and durability. (5) Penetrating oil: Based on linseed oil or tung oil, these finishes soak deeply into dense wood.

"penetrate deeper into the wood than water-based finishes," thus providing more and longer-lasting protection. On the other hand, water-based products are easier to clean up than oil-based products. They're also more forgiving of damp weather during installation, whereas an oil-based product requires bone-dry conditions before it can be applied to wood.

PENETRATING FINISHES

Unlike paints, penetrating finishes soak into the wood to preserve it and can stand up to foot traffic. Clear penetrating finishes are popular because they allow the natural grain of a wood

3   4   5

applied to the walls of a house, paint is superb. But on decking, it's a maintenance nightmare—paint just can't withstand invasion by prolonged water contact and abrasion by foot traffic. Similarly, clear film-forming products—classic varnishes and modern urethanes—are unmatched in their ability to bring out the beauty and depth of a wood surface while guarding against wear and tear. But they're often demanding to apply and always unforgiving of neglect when used outdoors: If not lightly sanded and recoated every one to three years, the film will begin cracking and peeling, and then must be stripped down to bare wood. These high maintenance requirements make them unfit for use on large expanses of decking.

But when you want to admire the warm look of a nicely varnished back door as you enjoy your deck, nothing beats marine spar varnish, the best varnish for outdoor use. The film is flexible enough to move with wood as it shrinks and swells. Knaebe recommends using a spar varnish containing UV absorbers and applying up to six thin coats for maximum protection. To keep the wood looking good, sand it lightly and brush on a fresh coat every year, or else the varnish will become brittle and crack. And if that happens, you'll have no choice but to scrape it all off and start over.

John Dee, a Massachusetts painter who has worked on *This Old House* projects, says that the decision about whether a clear film-forming finish is worth the trouble is one of aesthetics versus effort. "You need to really like the look of natural wood to be willing to do the maintenance."

deck to show through but aren't as good as pigmented finishes at blocking UV rays. Products range from clear sealers, which are simply nonpigmented penetrating finishes, to semitransparent and solid color stains.

Because they soak into the wood, penetrating finishes don't peel or require periodic scraping or sanding; the finish simply wears away. Compared with surface coatings, they do a better job of letting damp wood dry out, and they can be recoated without elaborate surface preparation. Little wonder that they've become so popular when it comes to decking. But even the best products need a routine, and sometimes even yearly, reapplication, and do little to guard the wood surface from dirt and wear.

FILM-FORMING FINISHES

Paint, of course, is the tried-and-true finish in this category. Rather than soaking into the wood, it forms a protective barrier on top of it. When

RIGHT: The stain on this deck was applied with a roller, allowed to set for 30 seconds, then wiped off. The process was repeated four times.

After nearly a decade of neglect, this redwood deck (LEFT) was restored to its original splendor (ABOVE) with little more than the right cleaner, a scrub brush, and a new coat of stain.

CHOOSING A PRODUCT

Knowing how finishes work is all well and good. The problem is, manufacturers jealously cloak their ingredients in secrecy, making it difficult for consumers to compare how much or which kind of pigments, UV absorbers, and preservatives there are in the can. To make matters worse, labeling requirements are maddeningly lax. For instance, the word "preservative" on a label means only that the government approved the relative safety of the fungicide and accepted evidence that it killed some organisms in whatever concentration it was tested. Manufacturers don't have to use this same concentration in their formulas, nor do they need to meet any standard for overall effectiveness.

Professionals who build and finish outdoor woodwork often favor products based on long experience. But about all a consumer can do is roughly infer the quality of a finish. You can do this by getting the Manufacturers Safety Data Sheet (MSDS), available from the retailer, and subtracting the solvent content (which has to be listed) from the total product amount. That will give you an approximate idea of the amount of solids—the ingredients that do the work—that will be left after the solvents evaporate. Another way to judge quality is by price: A cheap finish won't have a lot of the expensive ingredients that ensure durability.

PUTTING IT ON

Waiting nine months to a year before applying finish to a new preservative-treated-wood deck used to be standard procedure. Leaving wood unprotected for a while lowers the interior moisture content and allows the pores to open and accept more sealer or stain. Unfortunately, it also contributes to weathering, so its usually better to apply finish to a new (or newly cleaned) deck within a few weeks. Then apply a second coat the following year. "The second application leaves more finish in the wood," says Knaebe. "Then you can wait two or three years before putting on another coat."

The one exception to finishing right away is on new lumber that has a shiny-looking or burnished surface. This is called mill glaze, an artifact of the manufacturing process. Because it won't allow the finish to penetrate, anything you apply will peel off in a few months. You'll know it's there if water from a hose beads on the surface of unfinished wood. Wait two or three weeks so the surface can weather. If water still beads up, sand the area lightly before finishing.

CLEANING A DECK

It happens often enough: Deck planks that looked so fresh just a year ago suddenly seem, well, old, and nails in the posts appear to have cried charcoal tears. Although a deck endures an endless assault by the elements, a little patient cleaning and reconditioning will restore much of its former gleam. Some contractors pull out a pressure washer to blast off dirt and stains, but the gear must be used with great care and a deft touch to avoid damaging the wood. Many contractors, in fact, prefer to use commercial cleaning products.

Cleaning a deck: (1) Mildew buildup was washed away from the deck rails with a fine mist of household bleach. (2) A nylon-bristle brush and a solution of oxalic acid and water was used to scrub off dirt and superficial wood decay. (3) Cotton mitts slipped over latex gloves offer the best method for applying stain on hard-to-reach areas, while a painter's pad at the end of a long handle (4) lets you work stain into the decking without having to get down on your hands and knees.

Deck-cleaning products fall into two categories. *Cleaners* contain detergent and bleach, and work best at removing dirt and mildew. Bleach kills mildew on contact and brightens wood quickly. Though some finishing pros avoid bleach on the grounds that it can cause a finish to adhere poorly, most wood experts say that it is unlikely to cause damage when used sparingly and followed quickly by an ample rinse.

Restorers contain oxalic acid, also called wood bleach by some manufacturers. Oxalic acid strips away the unsightly black rust stains that form around ungalvanized nails and metal fasteners, and removes tannin streaks on cedar and redwood. Some finishing pros prepare their own restorer, mixing 12 ounces of powdered oxalic acid into a gallon of water and then scrubbing it into the planks.

AUTHORS: Max Alexander, Thomas Baker, Liz Ball, Nancy Beaubaire, Tom Connor, Jill Connors, Jeff Cox, John Decker, Dan DiClerico, Fran J. Donegan, Mark Feirer, Peter V. Fossel, Susan Green, Jeanne Huber, Hillary Johnson, Mervyn Kaufman, Anne Kruger, Wendy Marston, Michael McWilliams, Michael Morris, Bo Niles, Lynn Ocone, Donna Paul, Romy Pokorny, Curtis Rist, Cynthia Sanz, William G. Scheller, Warren Schultz, Nancy Stedman, Richard Stepler, Pat Stone, Helen Story, Terry Trucco, Joseph Truini, Amy Virshup, John D. Wagner, Logan Ward, Charles Wardell, Claire Whitcomb, Katherine Whiteside

PHOTOGRAPHERS: David Albanese, Eric Axene, Andre Baranowski, Timothy Bell, Matthew Benson, John Blais, Kay Boecker, Fran Brennan, Karen Bussolini, David Carmack, Kindra Clineff, John Decker, Roger Foley, Michael Grimm, Geoffrey Gross, Darrin Haddad, David Hamsley, Saxon Holt, Grace Huang, Keller & Keller, John Kernick, Mark Lohman, Michael MacCaskey, Michael Manuel, Ralph Masullo, Karen Melvin, Joshua McHugh, Tad Myers, John Nasta, Eric O'Connell, Benjamin Oliver, Craig Raine, Kevin Reardon, George Ross, Brian Smith, Kolin Smith, Robert Thien, James Worrell, Joe Yutkins

FRONT COVER: Michael Bates/English Country Garden Design

ILLUSTRATORS: Michael Freeman, Martin Mayo, Rodica Prato, Anthony Sidwell